THE
NATURE OF TRUTH

AN ESSAY BY

HAROLD H. JOACHIM
FELLOW AND TUTOR OF MERTON COLLEGE, OXFORD

GREENWOOD PRESS, PUBLISHERS
NEW YORK

BD
161
J6
1969

Originally published in 1906
by the Clarendon Press

First Greenwood Reprinting, 1969

Library of Congress Catalogue Card Number 69-13954

PREFACE

THE following Essay does not pretend to establish a new theory. Its object is to examine certain typical notions of truth, one or other of which—whether in the form of a vague assumption, or raised to the level of an explicit theory—has hitherto served as the basis of philosophical speculation. If I am not mistaken, every one of these typical notions and accredited theories of truth fails sooner or later to maintain itself against critical investigation. And I have tried, whilst exhibiting the nature and the grounds of their failure, to indicate in what direction (if in any) there appears some prospect of more successful construction.

The reader will find no mention of the theory known alternatively as 'Pragmatism' or 'Humanism'. It is not easy to discern the meaning of its advocates through the noise of their advocacy. But they appear to be engaged in a twofold enterprise. For firstly they desire to emphasize certain elementary theses, which many idealists are equally concerned to maintain; and these I have endeavoured to discuss, so far as the subject demanded, in my third and fourth chapters. But secondly they wish to revive certain views, which in Plato's *Theaetetus* are attributed to Protagoras. The revival is a reconstruction. The old wine is poured into new bottles; the ancient doctrine is arrayed in a modern dress. But in substance the doctrine remains, what Plato proved it to be : not a new theory of truth, but a denial of truth altogether.

It is natural to feel some hesitation in publishing a work avowedly critical in character and negative in result. But I offer this Essay to my fellow-students, in the hope that it will induce them to reflect once more on the foundations of their philosophical thinking. If they will but reflect in earnest, I shall be amply satisfied. For the conviction will force itself upon them that those foundations are fatally insecure. The ground will be cleared, and construction will come in due time.

Every writer on philosophical subjects is indebted, beyond all possibility of adequate acknowledgement, to the great thinkers of the past, and to those who are working with him in the field of his inquiry. But the debt is one which he makes for himself, or at least incalculably increases, by free and honest criticism. If the labours of those whom he criticizes have rendered his criticism possible, it is only by criticizing that he is brought to the intelligent appreciation of their work. Hence I must not be thought ungrateful or wanting in respect because I have criticized : nor must it be supposed that I am unmindful of those obligations which I have not expressly acknowledged. Thus, the reader will see for himself how greatly I have been influenced by Mr. F. H. Bradley and Professor Bosanquet, though I have referred to them but seldom, and then mainly in order to criticize. And

I am fully aware that the greater part of my work draws its inspiration from the writings of Hegel, whose name I have mentioned only once.

The whole of the second chapter was submitted to my friend Mr. Bertrand Russell before it was printed. I am most sincerely grateful to him for the patience and the kindness with which he replied to my criticism in detail. Since my primary object was to examine a typical theory of truth, and not to attack Mr. Russell, I have not thought it necessary to make any substantial alterations. But the reader must not assume that the theory which I have criticized is accepted by Mr. Russell as in all points identical with his own.

Lastly, I am glad to acknowledge the constant help and the many valuable suggestions which I have received from my friends Mr. J. A. Smith, Fellow of Balliol, and Mr. R. P. Hardie, Lecturer at Edinburgh University. And my thanks are specially due to the Master of Balliol, Dr. Edward Caird, who read the whole Essay and encouraged me to persevere in preparing it for publication.

CONTENTS

CHAPTER I

TRUTH AS CORRESPONDENCE

§ 1. IN most of the everyday judgements of common sense, and in many philosophical theories, a certain conception of truth is implied or expressed, which I shall call the 'correspondence-notion' of truth. Thus e.g. to 'speak the truth' is to speak 'in accordance with' or 'in conformity to' the facts. A 'true' man, or a 'true' friend, is a person whose outward acts 'correspond to'—faithfully reflect — his inner feelings. A narrative is 'true' if it 're-presents', in essentials and within its own sphere, the real order of events. So again, according to Aristotle, the synthesis or analysis of the thoughts expressed in a true judgement[1] must exactly re-present, or correspond to, the way in which the real things are conjoined or divided; and a 'scientific truth' is the conclusion of a deductive inference, which exactly repeats in its structure the necessary coherence of a substance with its *proprium* through the proximate cause of that connexion.

The above examples will serve to indicate the general type of theory which I call the 'correspondence-notion' of truth; and without further preliminaries I shall proceed to examine it.

2. Truth, according to all forms of the correspondence-notion, is a determinate relation between two

---

[1] The 'correspondence-notion' of truth in Aristotle is always confined to truth of judgement or inference. The immediate apprehension of Simple Realities is 'true' in a different sense. Cf. below, ch. iv, §§ 47, 48, and 50.

distinct factors : and this relation must be 'for' a
mind.[1]   In other words, truth is an experience of
two factors determinately related to one another.

It will be convenient to use Leibniz's conception of
the 'perceptive' state of a Monad, in order to bring out
the nature of the 'determinate relation' to which the
above description refers.   Every Monad is a unity of
an infinite inner plurality of qualitative differences.
And every qualitative difference, i. e. every element of
the inner manifold of each Monad, corresponds, or is
determinately and uniquely related, to an element of
the manifold in 'the world', i. e. in the other Monads.
In so far as a Monad is ·aware of the plurality which
it unrolls within itself, and aware that it thus corresponds, element for element, to a manifold other than
its own, the Monad consciously perceives ; and its
perception is true, and true for it.[2]   So far as the
Monad is not aware of its inner plurality as thus
corresponding, there is no 'perception' in the ordinary
sense of the term[3] ; and there is no truth 'for' the
Monad.   The Monad would 'reflect' the outer plurality, much as a mirror reflects an object.   But the
perception in the one case, and the reflection in the
other, would only exist 'for' a consciousness apprehending the two factors and their relation.   And apart
from this condition it would be meaningless to call
the Monad's inner state 'true' or 'false', or the

---

[1] It is possible (as we shall see) to hold a theory which denies
that 'truth' as such is 'for' any mind.   Truth, we may insist, is
'independent', and its nature must not be confused by the
irrelevant introduction of 'psychological' notions.   But we are
not at present concerned with this theory: see below, pp. 13, 35 ff.

[2] Leibniz calls such *conscious* perception 'apperception'.   The
reader will kindly bear in mind that I am not expounding
Leibniz's doctrine, but merely using it as a convenient illustra-
tion of the meaning of 'correspondence.'

[3] Leibniz calls it 'perception'; but he expressly extends the
use of the term for his own reasons.

mirror's disposition an 'accurate' or 'distorted' picture of the object.

The relation between the manifolds, it is hardly necessary to say, is neither bare identity nor simple otherness. In a sense, no doubt, it is 'the same' world, i.e. the same manifold, which constitutes the inner plurality of all the Monads. But each represents the universe with different degrees of clearness: each reflects the world from its own 'point of view'. The manifold, *qua* constituting the inner plurality of different Monads, is itself different. So it is not the same identical elements which appear both in the mirror and in the object. Yet the elements in the two factors, although not identical, are not barely other. For they are so related, that for each element on the one side there is a determinate element—one and only one—on the other. Correspondence, therefore, here means being related by a one-one relation.[1] Two factors, each a one-of-many, 'correspond' when each constituent of the one stands in a one-one relation to a determinate constituent of the other. And there is 'truth' when this correspondence is 'for' a consciousness; i.e. either 'for' one of the factors *qua* itself conscious, or 'for' a third being.

§ 3. Yet a closer inspection reveals fatal defects in the above account of the meaning of 'correspondence'. For (1) by reducing the corresponding factors to aggregates of simple elements, standing uniquely in relation one to one, we have created a mere semblance of clearness which criticism will show to be illusory; and (2) we have not even attempted to explain what 'being for a consciousness' is to mean.

(1) If you have a whole of parts such that each part contributes determinately to constitute the whole, and

---

[1] For the meaning of a 'one-one relation', see Mr. Bertrand Russell's *Principles of Mathematics*, I, pp. 113, 130, 305.

that the structural plan of the whole determines precisely the nature of the differences which are its parts[1], you can compare this whole with another whole of the same type.   And you can say 'the part x in A (the first whole) corresponds to the part y in B (the second whole)'.

Your judgement would mean that x fulfils in the inner systematization of A the same function as y fulfils in that of B: i. e. what x is to A, that y is to B. And if you could trace this analogy through all the parts of the two wholes, you would be justified in asserting that 'A corresponds to B', or that 'A and B are similar, or resemble one another'; or again that 'every part of A corresponds to every part of B', or that 'every part of A is related by a one-one relation to every part of B'.

The 'correspondence', when attributed to the wholes, is simply a name for identity of purpose expressed through materially different constituents as an identical structure, plan, or cycle of functions; and, when attributed to the parts, it means identity of function contributed by materially different constituents towards the maintenance of an identical plan or purpose.

Nothing is gained in clearness by the notion of a 'one-one relation' between the parts; for the relation in question depends through and through upon the system of relations—i. e. the plan, cycle of functions, or teleological scheme—within which the *relata* on either side have their being.   There is no 'correspondence' between two 'simple beings', nor between elements of wholes considered as 'simple beings', i.e.

---

[1] Such a whole is no mere aggregate or collection of its parts, but a genuine whole or individual.   And its unity will be teleological in character, i. e. its inner structure will be the systematic expression of a single plan, purpose, or idea.

without respect to the systematization of their wholes. And if this be so, it is clear that our effort to render the notion of correspondence precise was ill-advised. For we tried to reduce it to the notion of one-one relations between ultimately simple elements, or between constituents of wholes considered as ultimately simple atomic entities.   But a simple entity cannot *as such*, and considered *as such*, be related to anything. If we identify, distinguish, or in any way relate A and B— two simple entities—we have *eo ipso* retracted their simplicity; and their simplicity never existed, if their nature justified our proceedings.   A simple point on the surface of a mirror, *qua* simple point, can suggest nothing other than itself—if indeed it can be determinately 'itself' at all.   As a point on the surface, i.e. as one in a scheme of related points, it may under certain conditions 'suggest', 'resemble', 'correspond to', a different point in another system of related points whose structural scheme is the same as that of the scheme in the mirror.   But it has acquired its power of suggestion at the cost of its simplicity.

It will perhaps be objected that the above argument rests upon certain assumptions which modern Logic has shown to be mere superstitions.   And it is true that I have assumed (i) that a purely external relation is in the end meaningless and impossible; and (ii) that elements, which merely are juxtaposed or otherwise externally connected, do not so far constitute a genuine whole at all.   As regards the first assumption, I must admit that a relation, which really *falls between* two independent entities, is to my mind a third independent entity which in no intelligible sense relates the first two.   I am not indeed maintaining that every relation is *nothing but* the adjective of its terms.   But I am maintaining that every relation at least qualifies its terms, and is so far an adjective of them, even if

it be also something besides.   And I am maintaining
that, so far as A and B are related, they are *eo ipso*
interdependent features of something other than either
of them singly : and, on the other hand, that if A and
B really are each absolutely simple and independent,
it is nonsense to say that they also are really related.[1]
With regard to my second assumption, it is enough
for my present purpose to urge that at any rate
a judgement which claims truth, and a picture which
is to be a portrait, are wholes of parts whose unity is
not that of mere juxtaposition or external connexion.

We may now modify our account of 'correspondence'.   Two different factors, we shall say, 'correspond' when each of them is a whole whose inner
structure is teleological, when that structure is identical as the explication of the same idea or purpose,
and when, finally, for every distinctive part fulfilling
a determinate function within the one factor there is a
part fulfilling the same[2] function within the other.
In so far as the above conditions are completely
fulfilled, the wholes *exactly* correspond : and there is
correspondence, to some degree, in so far as the
conditions are fulfilled at all.   And if this correspondence is 'for' a mind, that mind regards the one
factor as a more or less accurate representation of the
other ; whilst if one factor is the judgement of a mind
about the other factor, that judgement is more or less
true according to the exactness of the correspondence.

§ 4. (2) The most difficult feature in the correspondence-notion has not hitherto been considered at
all—viz. the part which a mind is required to play in
the constitution of truth.   Either—as we have crudely
put it—one of the two corresponding factors must

---

[1] On 'external relations', see below, pp. 43 ff., 49.
[2] i.e. the part x in A contributes to A's being in the same way
as the part y in B contributes to B's being.

itself be 'the judgement of a mind about the other':
or the two factors in their correspondence must be
'for a mind'. In the latter case, there is on the
part of the mind a *recognition* of one factor as a true
description, a faithful portrait, an exact representation,
&c., of the other. In the former case, the mental
factor overreaches the other factor—i.e. the other
factor, as well as itself, is 'for it'—and there is on
the part of the mental factor a *recognition* of itself
as an adequate conception of, a true judgement or
inference about, the other factor. This—the more
complex case—is the one with which we are primarily
concerned: but we may hope that a fuller consideration
of the other more simple case will throw some light
upon it.[1]

It will be observed that in both cases I have spoken
of a *recognition* of the truth: and an obvious criticism
would be to insist on the separation of Truth and the
Recognition of it. 'Truth', it might be said, 'is the
correspondence of the two factors: and nothing further
is required. Whether a mind recognizes it or not, is
a purely psychological question and has nothing whatever to do with the logical problem as to the meaning
of truth. Truth is what it is independently, whether
any mind recognizes it or not. We do not make the
correspondence, which is truth; we find it, and our
finding is irrelevant to its being, and must be separated
therefrom by any sound theory.'

This is in fact the contention of a possible theory
to which we have already alluded [2], and we shall have
to examine it fully when we are criticizing that theory.
In the meantime, I shall assume that truth *is* essentially
in and for judgement. We do not create truth, but
only find it; and we could not find it if it were not

---

[1] The two cases, we shall find, come *in the end* to the same
thing. See below, pp. 18, 19.   [2] Above, p. 8, note 1.

there and (in a sense) independent of our finding. And yet we cannot separate truth and the finding of it, and treat these as two independent factors which are externally combined in the apprehension of truth. Truth, I shall assume, is not truth at all except in so far as it is recognized, i.e. except in so far as it is the living experience of a mind. And a 'correspondence' which is not 'for' a mind, whatever sense we may be able to give to such a notion, at any rate is not a truth. What makes the above criticism seem plausible is a certain ambiguity[1] which may be pointed out at once. The finding of a truth, as an historical process of (or in) *my* mind, is irrelevant to the nature and the being of the truth. A truth *is*, independently of *my* thinking it, and, again, in independence of the process through which I come to think it. But it does not follow, as the criticism assumes, that a truth *is*, independently of any and all thinking it, nor even in independence of any and all process of reaching it. 'The internal angles of a triangle are equal to two right angles': this is a truth, no matter whether you or I recognize it or not, and, in a sense, no matter whether any one is now thinking it. And, again, its truth does not depend upon the process through which I came to think it. And yet if no one thought it—if it had not come to be 'for' mind, and were not, in any sense, 'for' mind—'it' would not 'be' at all.

§ 5. Let us return to the consideration of the more simple case which we agreed to examine first. 'The two factors in their correspondence are for a mind': this is to be the meaning, when we (the mind in question) say of the one factor that it is a 'true description' or a 'faithful portrait' of the other. We perceive e.g.

---

[1] We shall be better able to see the full significance of this ambiguity when we come to treat of the individual and universal aspects of Truth. See below, §§ 7 and 8.

a human face and a portrait.   On each side we recognize
a whole of parts with a determinate inner structure or
plan of coherence.   The parts of the one whole are
materially different from the parts of the other; but
the structure of the two wholes, the form or plan of
coherence of their parts, is the same.   For every
determinate function in the maintenance of that plan
which is exercised by a part on the one side, there is
a determinate function the same in kind exercised by
a part on the other side.   Or again, we apprehend a
succession of historical events as a whole constituted
by the unfolding of an idea or the expression of
a purpose ; and, on the other hand, we apprehend a
chapter in a book in which this whole is 'repeated'
in a different material.   The latter we call a 'true
description' or a 'faithful narrative' of the former.

But in this account there is much that is unsatisfactory.   We have laid stress on the necessity of
teleological unity in both factors.   The face is to be
a whole whose parts contribute each a determinate
function to constitute and express its unity; it is, in
other words, to embody 'character' or 'significance'
for the mind apprehending it.   The historical succession
is to be apprehended as the unfolding of an idea or
the expression of a purpose.   It seems necessary to
insist on this condition ; for otherwise how could the
mind apprehend either factor as 'one', as a 'whole',
at all?   And how could it determine what are to
count as 'parts' on either side?   *One* event in
an historical succession is 'one' only by reference to
the purpose for which it is a means ; and one part
of the face is 'one', it would seem, as embodying
a determinate element in the character or significance
of the face.   But if we are driven thus to emphasize
the embodiment of purpose, the teleological structure,
in both factors, it seems clear that the 'truth' of

a narrative or a portrait—or even of a reflection—
becomes increasingly dependent on the nature of the
'recognition' by the apprehending mind.   We can no
longer suppose that the mind plays the part of the
absolutely disinterested spectator and *in no sense*
'makes' the facts.   On the contrary, the mind sees
what it makes by its interpretation : and the 'truth'
of the corresponding factor varies in degree with the
nature of the recognition which the mind brings to
bear.   What the painter sees in the face, *that* he
expresses in his portrait; and the portrait will be more
or less 'true' or 'faithful' according to the painter's
insight, and, again, according to the mind of the
spectator who sees and compares both the original and
the picture.   Even the photographer's camera can
'lie', i.e. fail to produce a 'true' representation of its
subject.   And though a chronicle may, from one point
of view, 'correspond' detail for detail with the
historical events, yet for its reader, even if not for
its writer, it may be radically false.   For it may
entirely miss the 'significance' of the piece of history,
and so convey a thoroughly false impression.

Thus the importance of 'correspondence', as the
constitutive condition of truth, sinks more and more
into the background.   Another condition emerges as
the primary determinant not only of the degree of
truth, but of its very being.   For truth is seen to
depend on the nature of the idea expressing itself
as the inner structure of the corresponding wholes,
rather than on the 'correspondence' of the two
expressions.   And of course we could not rest here.
For we cannot assume that the idea in question
possesses its 'significance' (its fullness of meaning
or its power to constitute truth) alone and in its own
right.   It in turn derives its significance from a larger
significant system to which it contributes.   And this

line of thought would lead us to a theory of truth fundamentally different from the 'correspondence-notion'. That notion, so far as we have studied it at present, appears to give us at best the mere externals of what constitutes truth. Correspondence, perhaps we may say, is a symptom of truth. We do not yet know whether there may be truth without correspondence; but at least there may be correspondence without truth, or with truth so trifling that serious falsehood is involved in it. And when there is truth, it is not the 'correspondence' which primarily determines its being, its nature, or its extent. Truth depends primarily on something other than correspondence—on something which itself conditions the being and the nature of the correspondence.

§ 6. And worse is to come. For we have now to consider the more complex case in which one factor, the 'mental' factor, recognizes itself as an adequate conception of, a true judgement or inference about, the other.

In the cases with which we have hitherto been concerned, one factor was recognized by a mind as representing the other: or the mind read both factors as conveying the same idea in different materials through 'corresponding' expressions. It was apparently more or less arbitrary *which* factor was the original and *which* the representation. In general we take the simpler or more abstract expression as the representation of the fuller, or more concrete, expression of the idea. Thus, the image in the mirror ' reflects' the face; and the image is a less concrete expression of the idea, an expression in a simpler material. The narrative 'portrays' the facts; and the narrative is a whole of simpler and abstract elements in comparison with the fullness and concreteness of the historical occurrences. In the two corresponding factors we have, it would seem, two more or less adequate embodiments of an idea—two partial expressions; and on the whole we treat the less adequate embodiment, the more incomplete expression, as the portrait or image of the more complete, though still partial, expression.[1]

But in the cases which we are now to consider, one factor is explicitly 'mental' in some sense in which the other is not; and the other factor is explicitly 'real' in some sense in which the first is not. And truth is to be the correspondence of the 'mental' with the 'real', so that the 'mental' apprehends the 'real'.

In the first set of cases there was an appearance of externality, of independence or objectivity, in the two corresponding factors which seemed to justify us in treating them apart from those cases which we have now to examine. The narrative and the events, the picture and the original, seem alike external to the apprehending mind; and the correspondence between the two factors, which that mind may observe, seems very different from that correspondence of judgement with reality which the judging mind constitutes as it judges. Yet really and in the end the two sets of cases come to the same thing and involve the same problem. For the truth of the narrative or the picture *is* only [2] for the mind which apprehends both narrative and events, both picture and original. And, as that mind's apprehension, the narrative and the picture are conceptions, judgements and inferences, which, in

[1] At times we appear to reverse this way of looking at things. For we may speak of a life as the faithful expression of certain principles or ideals, and even of a man as the 'living image' of his ancestor's portrait. But the antithesis between 'simple' and 'full', 'abstract' and 'concrete' expressions, as we have employed it above, is popular and indeterminate, and must not be treated seriously.

[2] I am not suggesting that the truth is *nothing but* the mind's apprehension, though *in a sense* this may turn out to be true.

contrast with the events and the original, are *somehow* distinctively 'mental'. The events and the original, on the other hand, are regarded *somehow*, in contrast with the narrative and the picture, as distinctively 'real'; although, as apprehended, they too are the experience of the same apprehending mind.

Thus both sets of cases involve the same problem, which we may formulate roughly in the following manner. Wherever there is truth, there are, according to the correspondence-notion, two expressions of an Idea, or two factors related in the fashion described above. And one factor is in some pre-eminent sense 'mental', the other in some distinctive way 'real'. Yet both factors are certainly 'mental', and also both factors are undeniably 'real'. What precise sense is to be given to the 'Mentality' and 'Reality' of the factors, so as to reconcile these apparently conflicting requirements?

A judgement e.g. is true, if the thoughts whose union is the judgement 'correspond' to the facts whose union is the 'real' situation which is to be expressed. *My* judgement is true if *my* ideas, as asserted by me in my judgement, correspond to the facts. But *my* ideas (as the corresponding factor) are 'real', and 'real' not simply in the sense that they are certain events actually happening in my psychical history. For it is not *qua* psychical events that my ideas correspond with the facts and, in corresponding, are true. And, on the other hand, the facts are 'mental'; for they are what the judgements of the world at large, or of the specialists in question, affirm—judgements with which I identify myself in the act of recognizing my private judgement as corresponding with the facts. Again, from the point of view of the 'world at large', or the 'body of scientific knowledge', truth is still, we are to suppose, a 'correspondence' between a 'mental' factor (certain thoughts, judgements, and inferences) and a 'real' something. And here at least it is recognized that the 'mental' factor is no mere psychical sequence, but is 'real' in a different sense; whilst it must be recognized on reflection that the 'real' factor is not 'external to mind' or 'unrelated to consciousness'. But it is not easy to learn, from the adherents of the correspondence-notion, *what* precisely the 'mental' factor is, and in what sense it is 'real'; or, again, *what* precisely the 'real' factor is, and in what sense it is related to consciousness, or to *what* consciousness it is related. Yet without a clear account of both these factors it is obvious that no definite meaning can be attached to the correspondence between them, which is truth.

§ 7. We may begin by reminding ourselves of a familiar distinction.[1]

Truth is clearly independent. It has its own stubborn nature, to which our thinking must conform on pain of failure, i. e. error. We do not make or alter truth by our thinking, any more than we make or alter goodness by our conduct, or beauty by our love or by our artistic endeavours. Truth is discovered, and not invented; and its nature is unaffected by the time and process of discovery, and careless of the personality of the discoverer. It is to this independent entity that the judgement of this or that person must conform if *he* is to attain truth. Correspondence of *his* thinking with this 'reality' is truth *for him*; but such correspondence requires an independent truth [2] as one of its factors and is not itself the essence of truth.

---

[1] Cf. e.g. F. H. Bradley 'On Truth and Practice', in *Mind*, N.S., No. 51, especially pp. 319, 320, 335.

[2] The 'real' factor here is the 'independent truth', i.e. truth recognized as independent by the individual who attains truth in making his judgement correspond.

And yet there is another side of the matter. For truth is actual as true thinking, goodness lives in the volitions and actions of men, and beauty has its being in the love of its worshippers and in the creative activity of the artist.[1] Truth, goodness, and beauty, in short, appear in the actual world and exist in finite experience. To experience them is, no doubt, to transcend the purely personal, the merely finite experience; but finite experience is the vehicle of their being. They live as the experience of finite subjects; and their life (at least on one side of itself) is judgement, emotion, volition—the processes and activities of finite individuals.

Truth, if it is to be *for me*, must enter into my intellectual endeavour and emerge in my conscious thought as the result of a personal process, and as, in a sense, *my* personal possession. I must get to know it, and I must express it when known, and the expression is tinged with my personal individuality and is *my* judgement. Doubtless it is irrelevant to the nature of truth whether *I* know it or *you*. Truth is independent of the process by which *I* come to know it, and is unaffected by the time at which I know it. But yet this independent truth itself, whose nature holds aloof from the conditions of its 'existence for me'—this truth, which I may struggle to grasp, but which in the very struggle retains its independence of my efforts

---

[1] Thus the beauty of a work of art—e.g. *Hamlet*, Beethoven's violin concerto, a great picture, or a statue—has its being partly in the experience of its creator, partly in the experience of those who appreciate it, and, in appreciating it, re-create it for themselves. The beauty of a poem, a play, or a piece of music clearly is dependent in a very vital sense upon the reciter, the actors, or the executant musician; but it is dependent also upon the emotional and intellectual individualities of the audience. The beauty of a picture or a statue *seems* independent of the individual interpretations of the lovers of beauty, but it is not so in reality, any more than it is independent of the artistic personality of its creator.

and is untouched alike by my success and by my failure—this independent truth lives and moves and has its being in the judgements of finite minds. It is independent of this and that mind, *qua* this and that ; independent of the particular time and process of its expression and the individual machinery of its revelation. But it is essential to it to be expressed or revealed, and to be expressed in the different features of its coherent structure as the knowledge of different minds. It is universal and single and timeless. But it is a single content or significance, which manifests itself in a plurality of meanings, in very different degrees at different stages of the development of human thought, and as a system of knowledge which constitutes and is constituted by the intellectual individualities of many finite thinkers.

§ 8. If we now return to the problem as to the corresponding factors, we may distinguish two cases ; for (1) *my* judgement is said to be 'true' when it corresponds to the 'facts' or the accepted views, and (2) a scientific theory or an accepted judgement is regarded as 'true' because it corresponds to the 'nature of things' or to 'Reality'.

It is clear that, where I claim truth for my private judgement as corresponding to the facts, both corresponding factors are before my mind.[1] But they need not both be 'for me' at the same level of consciousness. One factor is present to my mind—in the form

---

[1] For the sake of simplicity I am considering only the case in which my private judgement corresponds to the facts, i. e. is true, *for me*. If *you*—and not *I*—recognize that my judgement is true, the corresponding factors are 'before *your* mind'; and what is said in the text applies to the truth of my judgement *as it is for you*. My judgement is not true *for me*, in this case, any more than the likeness of the portrait or the reflection in the mirror are faithful or exact *for them*. The 'truth' of my judgement, when it is *for you* and not *for me*, falls into line with the cases of the mirror and the narrative. Cf. above, § 5.

perhaps of imperfectly articulate, vague, and more or less unmediated feeling—as the common environment which is 'the world' of myself and my fellows. The other factor is present to my mind—in the form of a reflective judgement—as the distinctly conceived synthesis of Thing and Property, Elements and Relation, Cause and Effect, &c. This second factor is the result of more or less definite analysis of some portion of the first; and, as thus involving a determinate operation of my mind, it is *par excellence* the 'mental' factor. Some subordinate portion of the first (or 'real') factor exhibits an inner structure which I recognize as repeated within the judged (or 'mental') factor. This identity of inner structure is the 'correspondence', which I call the 'truth' of my judgement.

If the above account is in outline correct, the 'facts', to which my judgement is to correspond, are the expression in and through my mind of that which is also expressed in and through the minds of my fellows. Thus I am divided in the experience which we call 'truth'; and, in respect to one side[1] of the division, I am the vehicle of a content which is universal and by no means merely my private affair. At the same time, though I am divided, I in the division overreach it. For I am aware of the two factors and of their correspondence; and I hold the personal or private nature of the one factor over against the impersonal or universal nature of the other, and compare the two. It is this identification of our full self with the content which we recognize as expressing itself in other selves, as well as with the content of our personal judgement, volition, or emotion, which gives to all human experience, speculative, moral, and artistic, its paradoxical character. And it is the recognized universality of the content of

---

[1] i.e. in respect to one side *at least*. The same holds with regard to the other side also, as we shall see directly (below, § 9).

the 'real' factor which constitutes its 'reality' for me, and gives it the independent and constraining force in virtue of which I test the truth of my judgement by it and not its 'reality' by my judgement.

So much, perhaps, may be admitted as a rough description of the conditions under which I claim truth for my judgement. But the 'correspondence-notion' attempts to render this description more precise by offering a definite theory as to *the nature of the test* which my judgement must satisfy if it is to be true. The test, according to it, is identity of structure within the two factors. My judgement is true (is rightly regarded by me as true) if it, as a whole of parts, exhibits an inner strûcture identical with the inner structure of the 'real' factor, or of some subordinate whole within that factor.

§ 9. It is this determinate theory as to the nature of the test which characterizes the correspondence-notion ; and on this determinate theory, as we have now to see, that notion is wrecked.

We have, in the first place, wrongly assumed that the 'mental' factor is purely personal; and we have wrongly contrasted it with the 'real' factor as purely universal. The contrast cannot be maintained so sharply. For the 'real world', which forms the felt background of myself and my fellows, enters into, or *is*, the experience of each of us in a fashion uniquely tinged with our respective individualities. And on the other hand, the 'mental' factor, i.e. the reflective synthesis of elements consciously analysed which is my judgement, is never 'purely personal'. The 'purely personal' would be strictly incommunicable; but judgements, even 'my private opinions', are essentially communicable, and every element and feature of them is, on one side of itself, the common inheritance of many or all of us. And, in any case, the 'mental' factor, however private and personal, is *for me* an object distinguishable and distinguished from 'myself', and so far universalized.

This defect in our account may, however, easily be remedied. It is mainly a question of emphasis. Everything, we may agree, which is in any sense 'real', possesses the dual character of universality and unique individuality; and without this dual character nothing can enter into our experience. But the 'common content', the 'universal idea', the 'world' or whatever we call this dual matter of experience, expresses itself doubly in my consciousness when I judge. And 'truth' means the correspondence between these two expressions, each of which is a more or less imperfect embodiment of the dual content expressed.[1] In one expression the content is imperfectly individualized, and appears for me in the form of vague unmediated feeling; in the other expression it is imperfectly universal in the form of 'my own private' opinion.

But, in the second place, we have made an assumption which we cannot justify; and yet, without it, we cannot maintain the correspondence-notion. For we have been forced to regard correspondence as identity of structure, and to attribute truth to my judgement because it repeats in its internal organization the inner structure of the 'real' factor, or of some subordinate whole within that. Now if there is *no* difference in the two factors, there clearly is no 'correspondence'—there is identity. But if there is a difference, e.g. what we loosely called a 'material' difference[2], how can there also be identity of structure? For 'structure' is a name for scheme of inner relations, and relations which really relate different elements cannot be identical, i.e. cannot be identical if the

---

[1] Cf. above, § 5, p. 16.　　　　[2] Above, § 3, p. 10.

differences of the elements are differences of them *qua* related. Or we may put the matter less abstractly. On the one side we have a whole of experience at the level of feeling; and, on the other side, a whole of experience at the level of reflective thought. To say that there is (or may be) identity of structure is to maintain that these experiences are different matters subsumed under an identical form. And whatever may be said of such a conception in general, at least it does not do justice to the unity of an experience-whole. Whatever may be the case with other 'wholes', at least a felt-whole, or again a thought-whole, are not elements *together with* a scheme of relations. *Such* wholes at least cannot be analysed into materials subsumed under an external form—i. e. a form which can be what it is, unaffected by the differences of the material which it unifies.

For the present we must leave the matter here. A full discussion would in the end turn on the problem of the possibility of 'purely external relations', which provisionally we have agreed to deny.[1] If that denial be maintained in respect to the relations within such wholes as are in question—*a fortiori*, if it be maintained in regard to all relations without restriction—it follows that the correspondence-notion must be rejected. It may be a convenient working hypothesis under which to think of the 'truth' of my judgement, but it cannot pretend to be an adequate account of what 'truth' in such cases means.

We have still to consider the second case mentioned above [2], and we can then sum up our results.

§ 10. A scientific theory, or an accepted judgement, is regarded as 'true' because it corresponds to the 'nature of things' or to 'Reality'.

[1] Cf. above, § 3, pp. 11, 12 ; and see below, pp. 43 ff., 49.
[2] § 8, p. 22.

The truth of *my* judgement, as we considered it in § 8, depended upon its 'correspondence' with a universal content which was present to me in the form of feeling. We have seen that the precise meaning of this correspondence will not bear investigation ; but at any rate there seems in this case a more or less definite sense in the antithesis between a primarily-universal and a primarily-individual factor.[1]

But assuming that *my* judgement has, for myself and for others, substantiated its claim to truth in the sense that it is recognized and adopted by all intelligent people, we have an 'accepted judgement' or a 'scientific theory'. And here again the correspondence-notion steps in, and invites us to agree that truth means correspondence between the judgement and 'Reality' or the 'nature of things'.

The 'mental' factor here, i.e. the judgement, is unambiguously a logical content or meaning. Its psychological aspect, its 'existence' as the actual judgements of particular persons, is ignored as irrelevant. If awkward questions are asked, we shall probably be told that it is the expression of 'intelligence as such' or of the 'universal consciousness'; or that it is 'what every one must and does think under certain assumptions'. Assuming e.g. certain definitions and axioms, the systematic outcome of which is known as 'Euclidean Space', every one must judge that 'the internal angles of a triangle are together equal to two right angles'. Under those assumptions this judgement

---

[1] We might have looked for the truth of *my* judgement in its correspondence with other people's judgements. But (*a*) the mere fact that many people hold (or express) the same or similar opinions cannot make those opinions true ; and (*b*) this fact must be *for me*, if I am to claim truth for my judgement in virtue of its correspondence with theirs. And it can be *for me*, in the end, only in the form explained, viz. as a more or less unmediated feeling, an atmosphere invading all of us.

is a truth for all. It is a necessary element in a scientific theory of Euclidean Space; divergence from it is error.

But what is the 'Reality', correspondence with which constitutes the truth of this judgement? If you say 'Euclidean Space', I answer that 'Euclidean Space' itself is a system of such judgements, and that the truth of each of them is constituted by its coherence with all the others, but not by its 'correspondence' with anything external to the system. And if you say 'The real extended world is the Reality in question', is this not a mere name for the confused unmediated experience of which the clear articulate expression is the system of Euclidean geometry? If so, the position in which we found ourselves in §§ 8 and 9 is repeated, and we are driven to the same conclusion.[1]

§ 11. We may now sum up results and report progress. We found that the notion of 'correspondence' implied two factors, each of which was a whole-of-many cohering teleologically; and thus 'correspondence' seemed to become identity of structure, or plan of organization, in different materials. Taking 'correspondence' in this sense, we saw that the nature of the structure, or the purpose or idea which it unfolded, emerged more and more into importance as the essence of truth, whilst the fact of correspondence showed itself as at most a symptom of truth. A true description or a good portrait seemed to depend for their truth upon the fullness of the significance embodied for the apprehending mind in the two expressions; and this result, as we pointed out, would lead to the notion of truth as determined by systematic coherence. We had previously decided to reject for the present the view that truth is a quality of something real without any relation to its recognition by mind (§§ 2–5).

[1] For a fuller treatment see below, chapter 3, part ii.

We then passed on to consider the correspondence-notion as it would apply to 'true' judgement. We found that here one of the factors was explicitly 'mental', and that it was vital to determine in what sense it was both 'mental' and 'real', and again in what sense the other factor was *par excellence* 'real' and yet not unrelated to mind (§ 6). In order to deal with this problem, we found it necessary to call attention to the dual nature of human experience, its universality and independence, and yet also its individuality and its dependence on personal and private conditions (§ 7). We then endeavoured to express the nature of the two factors, in the case of a judgement of mine claiming truth, in terms of the result of this discussion. We found that when they are so expressed their antithesis (as 'mental' and 'real') possesses a more or less intelligible meaning. But we discovered that the idea of an identical structure in different materials is quite inadequate when applied to the wholes in question, viz. felt- and thought-wholes. And thus the whole notion of correspondence, however useful as a working hypothesis, breaks down if regarded as an adequate conception of truth (§§ 8, 9). Finally we considered the case in which a universally accepted judgement, or a scientific theory, is supposed to be 'true' because corresponding to Reality. And we found that here again the notion of correspondence must give place to the idea of systematic coherence (§ 10).

Our next task, therefore, would naturally be to examine the view of truth as coherence. But, before we do so, we ought to try to clear certain difficulties out of the way. For (1) we have said nothing, or nothing explicitly, about sensation. And yet, it will be urged, the strength of the correspondence-notion lies in its agreement with the common-sense view of sensation. In sensation we are in contact with Reality. *There* we come face to face with a stubborn, independent, controlling Real; and truth, in its primary and most obvious sense, means correspondence or conformity of our ideas to the facts given to us in sensation. And (2) we must endeavour to dispose of a view which has long been haunting us : the view that truth and falsity are qualities of certain entities entirely independent of mind.

CHAPTER II

TRUTH AS A QUALITY OF INDEPENDENT ENTITIES

§ 12. OUR object in the present chapter is to examine certain views which threaten to invalidate our previous conclusions and to bar the way to our further progress. In § 11, we arranged these views under two heads. There was (1) a certain theory as to the nature of sensation, on which the correspondence-notion was to be irrefutably established; and (2) there was a certain theory as to the nature of truth, which had nothing whatever to do with the correspondence-notion. We shall see, however, that both of our enemies draw their forces from a common base; and it is with that base that we shall be primarily concerned. A common assumption is made by both, and from that assumption development proceeds in two different ways. But one of the developments is more or less accidental, whilst the other is the necessary logical extension of the assumption. In the accidental development, the common assumption is employed as a foundation for the correspondence-notion of truth. The other development leads to a theory of truth so different from any of the prevailing views that, in endeavouring to state it, I may be accused of setting up a crude and ridiculous travesty. And the difficulty of a fair statement is increased by the fact that this new theory involves, and also supports, a radically new Logic and Metaphysics. Thus, in order fully to appreciate it, we should have to enter into a new philosophical universe.

So far as I know, there does not at present exist any systematic exposition of the new Logic and Metaphysics. The nearest approach to a complete exposition is to be found in the works of Mr. Bertrand Russell. In his *Philosophy of Leibniz*, in various articles in *Mind*, and in his *Principles of Mathematics*, he constantly applies the principles of the New Philosophy to the solution of the problems with which he is concerned, and to the criticism of current philosophical views. But—no doubt quite rightly—he neither offers, nor professes to offer, a systematic exposition of the Logic and Metaphysics whose principles he is applying. We are given to understand, in general, that there *is* such a system, which will emerge (or perhaps has emerged) triumphant from the gulf of criticism which has swallowed all other philosophies. But at present we have to construct this new system for ourselves out of Mr. Russell's applications of it, and such construction is necessarily precarious. At times, indeed, Mr. Russell refers us to the writings of Mr. G. E. Moore. But although Mr. Moore's *Principia Ethica*, and his articles in *Mind* and elsewhere, contain interesting indications (and more or less fragmentary expositions) of a new Logic and Metaphysics, I have not been able to discover in them anything like a systematic account.

Under these circumstances I have thought it worth while to discuss, so far as possible without personal reference and without personal controversy, a theory of truth which seems to me both important and erroneous—and important mainly because of the nature of its erroneousness. The theory in question has been suggested to me by the writings of Messrs. Russell and Moore, and I gratefully acknowledge my obligation. But although I have made a free use of their writings, and have not scrupled to employ their

terminology wherever it seemed convenient, I have
no desire to attribute to them a view which perhaps
they do not hold. nor to impute to them those logical
and metaphysical positions on which that view, as
I conceive it, depends.   Still less must the reader
suppose that the logical affiliation here ascribed to
that view—its derivation from the assumption that
'experiencing makes no difference to the facts'—either
is, or would be, recognized by Messrs. Russell and
Moore.   For my purposes it is irrelevant whether any
philosopher actually holds the view which I am about
to discuss.   It seems to me to follow logically from
an assumption which is commonly made, and to
involve certain logical and metaphysical principles
which are worth examining.   Occasionally I have
criticized statements quoted *verbatim* from Mr. Russell, because they seemed to me the best expositions
and illustrations of the type of theory in question.
But though I may thus have been led to adopt at
times a polemical tone, and to attack the views of an
actual philosopher, my primary object is to conduct
an *impersonal* examination of a certain assumption and
an *impersonal* criticism of certain logical and metaphysical principles.

§ 13. In sensation—so we are to assume—we are
in direct contact with the Real.   The Real is indeed
'given' to us, and it is also 'accepted.'   But what
is given to us in sensation is independent of the
acceptance and of the recipients, and is, in that
independence, the stubborn authority which controls
in the end all our thinking, feeling, and doing.   The
Real in sensation is present to a sentient consciousness : for 'sensation' is a complex, which includes
'something' and also the 'awareness' thereof.   But
the nature of the Real is in no way affected by
its presence to the sentient consciousness : i. e. our

'acceptance', if it is not purely passive, at least in no way modifies the 'something' which we accept. Sensation—the sentient apprehension of a sensible quality—must be analysed into two simple factors and a relation. The factors are (1) the Quality—a simple, timeless, unchangeable, independent Real; and (2) the Apprehension—something 'mental' or 'psychical'. And if we would avoid the errors of Idealism, we must remember that, although in the complex these factors are united by a relation, each factor *is* (and remains what it is) independently of the other. Thus it is the first duty of any sound philosophy to separate the factors, and to study each strictly by itself. As to the *relation*, we must observe that it is a unique, not further definable, relation. It is that peculiar, distinctive relation which obtains between 'subject' and 'object' in Experience; and its character is such that it holds the related factors together, and yet also leaves them completely untouched and unaffected by the union.[1]

The above 'assumption' is simply a plain statement of the facts. It will be welcomed by common sense, and it will clear the most formidable difficulties out of the path of philosophy. And, *first*, we may indicate how it is to be used in defence of the correspondence-notion of truth. By analysis of our sentient experience we can separate out the indubitably Real; and this is the ultimate standard, correspondence with which constitutes truth. When we talk of the 'facts of the case', of the 'actual historical events', of the 'original' of a portrait, or of 'the nature of things' which science is to represent, we mean, in the last resort, this Real given in sensation. No doubt this Real, as we experience it, is always given in relation to our apprehension, and always in conjunction and combination with

[1] Cf., however, below, p. 50, note.

much that is 'the work of the mind'. But we must separate out what is 'given' from that which is super-imposed upon it ; and again we must cut this purified 'given' clear from the manner of its acceptance and the nature of the recipients. The work of separation and dissection is hard, but not impossible ; and the residuum is a standard whose independent Reality is beyond suspicion.

The only adequate answer to this defence of the correspondence-notion is the criticism of its assumption ; and I shall enter upon that presently. But, in the meantime, it should be noticed that, *even granting the assumption*, some of the chief difficulties in the corre-spondence-notion are still unsolved. For, assuming the unchangeable and independent Real immediately given in sensation, *what* is to correspond to it, and what is the nature of the correspondence ? Is the 'mental factor' (e.g. in a 'true' system of judgements) a complex tissue woven with mental schemata of syn-thesis out of psychical replicas of the Real given in sensation ? Or are there no psychical replicas, no mental counterparts of the given Real ? and is the 'mental factor' a mere form, a mere scheme of prin-ciples of synthesis ? It seems necessary to adopt one of these two alternatives ; and yet, whichever we choose, 'correspondence' is meaningless. For the 'mental factor' either is entirely, or essentially contains, a formative structure which *just is not* the structure of the Real. And 'correspondence', as we saw, requires identity of structure in the corresponding factors.

We may *next* proceed to develop our 'assumption' in a far more radical fashion ; and, cutting ourselves loose from the correspondence-notion altogether, we may formulate a new theory of truth.

§ 14. For, if we can sever the 'Real' in sensation from everything 'mental', we are logically entitled to go further. It is ridiculous to suppose that my vision makes the greenness of the tree, or my hearing the harmony of the chord. No doubt, *to be experienced,* the greenness must be seen, and the harmony must be heard. But the fundamental postulate of all Logic is expressed in our 'assumption': viz. that the 'experiencing' makes no difference to the facts. The notes of the chord are in harmony, or the harmony is *there,* whether I hear them or not. No matter whether I see it or not, the tree is green. Its greenness is *there,* an independent unchangeable[1] fact. Now the same holds in principle of Judgement and Inference. For it is ridiculous to suppose that the equality of the interior angles of a triangle to two right angles is made by me in the judging; or that this 'truth' became true when the first geometer discovered it, and would cease to be true if no one believed it. No doubt, *to be experienced,* the equality must be judged, or in some way apprehended. But we must sever the psychical apprehension from the 'truth' apprehended. The 'truth' is *there,* timelessly, unchangeably, independently itself; a complex, whose simple constituent elements yet eternally and inseparably cohere to form a single entity. Such an entity is possessed of a genuine unity; since, although for analysis it is complex, it cannot be compounded out of the simple elements which analysis reveals as its constituents. It may be called a 'Proposition', to distinguish it alike from the simple entities (e. g. the real qualities, which are given in sensation), and from that which current Logic calls a 'Judgement'. A 'judgement', in ordinary logical usage, is a hybrid, in which psychical elements (such as belief, apprehension, &c.) are unwarrantably blended with the purely logical fact, the

---

[1] The tree may cease to be green, but the 'greenness' itself is eternal and unchangeable.

complex and yet single entity which we have called a ' Proposition '.

' Truth ' and ' Falsity ', in the only strict sense of the terms, are characteristics of ' Propositions '. Every Proposition, in itself and in entire independence of mind, is true or false ; and *only* Propositions can be true or false. The truth or falsity of a Proposition is, so to say, its *flavour*, which we must recognize, if we recognize it at all, immediately : much as we appreciate the flavour of pineapple or the taste of gorgonzola.[1] ' Knowledge ' is a complex, involving true propositions and belief : i.e. it is the appreciation of the flavour of these entities, combined with retention of the true and rejection of the false propositions. And ' Error ' is a complex, involving false propositions and belief : i.e. it is the misappreciation of flavours, combined with rejection of the true and retention of the false propositions. The true and the false—i.e. propositions, their eternal relations, their combination into inferences, &c., &c.—are the subject-matter of Logic. Psychical phenomena—e.g. belief, apprehension, &c.—are the subject-matter of Psychology. Knowledge and Error are the subject-matter of Epistemology, a complex science involving both Logic and Psychology.

Can we further describe the difference between true

[1] Cf. Russell, *The Principles of Mathematics*, I, Preface, p. v. ' The discussion of indefinables—which forms the chief part of philosophical logic—is the endeavour to see clearly, and to make others see clearly, the entities concerned, in order that the mind may have that kind of acquaintance with them which it has with redness or the taste of a pineapple.' (Cf. *ib*. p. 129.) What is here said of the primary propositions, or ' indefinables ', appears to be extended elsewhere to *all* propositions. Cf. Russell on ' Meinong's Theory of Complexes and Assumptions ' (III), in *Mind*, N.S., No. 52, p. 523 : ' It may be said—and this is, I believe, the correct view—that there is no problem at all in truth and falsehood ; that some propositions are true and some false, just as some roses are red and some white ; that belief is a certain attitude towards propositions, which is called knowledge when they are true, error when they are false.' Cf. also *ib*., p. 524.

and false propositions ? Both, as we have seen, are eternal unchangeable entities : and it seems as if there were nothing more to be said, except that they just *do* differ, precisely *qua* true and false. The difference is immediate, must be apprehended intuitively, and there is an end of the matter. Yet we may endeavour to carry our analysis a little further. For a true proposition, we may say, involves an element which is not contained in a false proposition ; and it is this additional element which constitutes its truth. The element in question attaches to the Proposition in itself : i.e. is a constituent of its being for Logic, and not for Psychology. We may adopt Mr. Russell's terminology, and call this element ' assertion ', if we remember that it is ' *assertion* ' *in a strictly logical and non-psychological sense*—whatever that may mean. The presence of the same element will serve to distinguish a genuine Proposition (e.g. ' Caesar died ') from the content of a Proposition from which the life of the Proposition has vanished (e.g. ' Caesar's death ').[1]

---

[1] Cf. Russell, *Principles of Mathematics*, § 38. ' The question is : How does a proposition differ by being actually true from what it would be as an entity if it were not true ? It is plain that true and false propositions alike are entities of a kind, but that true propositions have a quality not belonging to false ones— a quality which, in a non-psychological sense, may be called being *asserted*. Yet there are grave difficulties in forming a consistent theory on this point, for if assertion in any way changed a proposition, no proposition which can possibly in any context be unasserted could be true, since when asserted it would become a different proposition. But this is plainly false ; . . . Leaving this puzzle to logic, however, we must insist that there is a difference of some kind between an asserted and an unasserted proposition.' Cf. also § 52 : ' But there is another ' [i.e. non-psychological] ' sense of assertion, very difficult to bring clearly before the mind, and yet quite undeniable, in which only true propositions are asserted. True and false propositions alike are in some sense entities, and are in some sense capable of being logical subjects ; but when a proposition happens to be true, it has a further quality, over and above that which it shares with false propositions, and it is this further quality which is what I mean

§ 15. The theory of truth which has just been sketched rests upon an assumption claiming to express 'the fundamental postulate of all Logic'. Once grant that 'experiencing makes no difference to the facts', and the theory inevitably follows. And you cannot refuse to grant a principle of this kind—so it may be urged—if you are to have a Logic at all.[1] It is difficult to argue convincingly against such a position. For if an assumption *is* the basis of all Logic, then arguments directed against it appear, by a very natural confusion, to be *eo ipso* devoid of logical cogency. The assumption, in fact, gets established by a kind of ontological proof.

I shall, however, endeavour to show: (1) that the assumption, in any sense in which it is true, is irrelevant to the theory of truth which professes to be based on it; whilst, on the other hand, the assumption, in the sense in which that theory uses and interprets it, is false ; (2) that if, accordingly, this assumption be rejected, the theory has to choose between two disagreeable alternatives. For *either* the 'independent truth' will be and remain entirely in itself, unknown and unknowable ; *or*, if known or knowable, the truth will become a private and personal possession, dependent for its being upon an individual intuition which itself is a particular psychical existent—and thus the theory will have defeated its own object, which was to vindicate the independence of truth.

(1) 'Experiencing makes no difference to the facts. Sensating, conceiving, judging, leave untouched and independent the Real Qualities sensated, and the

by assertion in a logical as opposed to a psychological sense. The nature of truth, however, belongs no more to the principles of mathematics than to the principles of everything else. I therefore leave this question to the logicians with the above brief indication of a difficulty.'

[1] Cf. above, § 13, p. 33 ; § 14, p. 36.

Entities conceived or judged.' How are we to interpret
this statement? It is tolerably plain from the illustrations[1] how 'experiencing' is interpreted. It is *my*
vision, *my* hearing, *my* judging—i. e. the actual sensating, the actual thinking, of a particular subject at a
particular time—which are to 'make no difference to
the facts'. The tree is green, the notes form a har-
monious chord, the angles are equal to two right
angles, whether I, or you, or Euclid, or any individual
subject, is or is not actually experiencing them.

It is not so plain how we are to interpret ' the facts',
to which no difference is made. 'Greenness', 'Harmony', 'Equality' are to remain eternally and
unalterably themselves, whether they are also experienced or not. They are 'the facts', and they *are*
there independently and in themselves. But what is
their *being there*? Not, on the theory, 'their being
experienced'; for that is to mean their 'being actually
sensated or judged', a mere adventitious accident of
their *being there*. Then does it mean 'their being as
objects of possibly-actual sensating and judging'? Is
greenness e. g. *there*, in the sense that it is such that,
under determinate conditions, there is an actual
sensated green, or an actual sensating of green? But
this would imply, in the 'independent facts', an
essential relatedness, not indeed to *my* sensating or
thinking *qua* 'this' and 'mine', but to sensating and
thinking as the common modes in which I and you and
other individual subjects manifest their being as
conscious. And an 'essential relatedness' would
mean that 'the facts', in and by themselves, *are not*
there at all; that what *is there* is something within
which the so-called 'facts' are a partial factor, dependent for its being and nature on another factor, and
incapable of being 'in itself' or independent. And

[1] Above, § 14, p. 36.

this other factor is of the nature of 'experiencing', though it is not *my* experiencing *qua* 'this' and 'mine'.

Either, then, we shall have to say that the *being there* of the facts is their combining with another factor (of the nature of 'experiencing') to constitute a whole, whose factors involve one another; and this interpretation destroys the relevancy of the assumption. For, if our theory of truth is to follow, the facts must be entirely in themselves and independent. *Or* we shall have to maintain that the whole constituted by 'the facts' and 'experiencing' (in any sense of the term) is no genuine whole, but a mere external adjustment. The two factors are, or may be, related; but the relation when, or as, it obtains, leaves each precisely what it was, viz. absolutely in itself and independent. The assumption, as thus interpreted, is relevant, and the theory proceeds. But as thus interpreted the assumption is false, conflicts with common sense, and is in the end unmeaning.

For let us consider. Greenness[1] *is there*, in itself; and, though it may be sensated, its relation to the sentient consciousness leaves it *in the relation* precisely what it was when not so related, and what it will be again when no one is sensating it. Now this does not mean merely that greenness is essentially the same, whether *I* see it or *you* see it: i. e. as the common content of percipient consciousness of the human type. Nor does it mean that greenness, whether *I* conceive it or *you*—i. e. as the common content of human abstract thought—is the same concept. All this may be true; but it is not relevant. The theory maintains that greenness is what it is in complete independence of any and all forms of experiencing, and indeed of everything other than itself. It means that greenness neither

---

[1] I use the term 'greenness' to mean the eternal unchangeable quality 'green', in distinction from *this* or *that* instance of green.

itself is, nor ever enters as a factor into, a whole such that the determinate natures of its constituents reciprocally involve one another. Greenness is, for the theory, an ultimate entity in the nature of things, which has its being absolutely in itself. How, under these circumstances, greenness can yet sometimes so far depart from its sacred aloofness as to be apprehended (sensated or conceived); and how, when this takes place, the sensating or conceiving subject is assured that its immaculate *perseitas* is still preserved —these are questions to which apparently the only answer is the dogmatic reiteration of the supposed fact: ' It is so ; and if you cannot see it, you are wanting in philosophical insight.' But the plain man, as well as the philosopher, has his ' insight '. He will tell you that greenness is to him a name for a complex fact, the factors of which essentially and reciprocally determine one another. And he will say that if you choose to select one factor out of the complex, and to call it ' greenness ', there need be no dispute about the term ; but, as thus isolated, your greenness is an abstraction, which emphatically, in itself and as such, is not *there* nor *anywhere*. If you appeal to your doctrine of a 'unique relation', and urge that greenness *both* ' is there ' in itself and *also* is (at times or always) in relation to sentient or conceptual consciousness, he will ask you how you reconcile this ' both ' and ' also '. He will question in what sense it is *the same* greenness, which is *both* in itself and *also* in relation to something else. And, if you deny that there is here anything to reconcile, he will appeal to *his* ' insight '. Who shall say that *his* is the insight of a lying prophet, whilst *yours* bears the divine stamp of truth ?[1]

---

[1] It is no answer, from the point of view of the theory in question, to say : ' Our insight is justified by the consistency of the system of judgements into which it develops.' For if syste-

§ 16. It is worth while, perhaps, to pursue the criticism of this assumption a little further. Greenness is an entity in itself. And though, as experienced, it is related to a sentient consciousness, yet even in that relation it remains in itself and unaffected by the sentience. Is it then entirely irrelevant to the nature of greenness what the nature of the sentience may be? Clearly, the sentience to which greenness can be related is 'vision', not 'hearing'. But we are to understand that this restriction is not based on the nature of greenness as such, but is just a fact. And presumably also the restriction in the range of the sentience—the restriction, e.g. of vision to colour, of hearing to sound, of this type of vision to greenness, &c.—is just a fact, which in no way enters into the nature of the sentience. Vision and greenness come together, and we have a 'seeing of green', or a 'sensated green'; but the meeting of the two is cool and unconcerned, and indicates no affinity in their natures. Their meeting is one of those ultimate inexplicabilities of which—on some theories at any rate—the Universe is full.

The *de facto* restriction in the range of *relata* on either side seems, indeed, to go much further. For, on the one hand, greenness does not manifest its independent and simple nature to the vision of every subject: a colour-blind subject e.g. sees (or thinks he sees) 'redness'. Even within the 'normal' vision [1], it seems given to very few—to a 'philosopher' here and there—to see *the* self-identical simple Quality, which

matic consistency, or coherence, is to be the test of truth, the whole position is abandoned. 'Truth' is then no longer an immediate quality of Propositions in themselves. On the appeal to 'Insight', see below, §§ 18 and 19.

[1] What 'normal' means, for the theory which we are considering, is a difficult question. Is 'the normal vision' that of the majority? Or is the normality, e.g. of *my* vision, guaranteed to me by immediate inspection?

is greenness. The painter sees many different greennesses where the untrained eye sees but one. And if
the painter finds a name for each different shade, and
recognizes each as an ultimate simple Quality, who
will guarantee that his discrimination is both legitimate and adequate; that each of his Simples is really
different from all its neighbours, and that none of his
Simples can possibly itself prove manifold?

On the other hand, that my vision here and now
should be a vision of greenness and not e.g. of redness; still more that it should be a vision of the ultimate simple greenness, and not of a confused complex
of many undiscriminated shades of greenness: this,
if it takes place, takes place by a miraculous *de facto*
coincidence. And it requires a correspondingly miraculous 'insight' to assure me that it takes place.

We may at this point detect in the New Philosophy
a strong family likeness to an extreme Occasionalism,
without the *Deus ex machina* to render Occasionalism
plausible. Sentience has been pulverized into atomic
sensatings, and the object or sphere of sentience into
atomic Qualities. Atom on one side comes together with
Atom on the other side; but why *this* Atom should
be related to *that*, or indeed any Atom to any other,
is a question which cannot be answered. It cannot
be answered, for there is no rational ground for the
relation. The meeting, the relation, between *this*
Atom and *that* is a coincidence, which just happens
or which *de facto* is. We must take it on faith; for
we are told that it is, and those who tell us tell us
also that they are possessed of philosophical insight.[1]

---

[1] Cf. Russell, 'Meinong's Theory of Complexes and Assumptions' (III), *Mind*, N.S., No. 52, p. 519: 'And this theory would
render more intelligible *the curious fact that the apprehension of
simples, so far from being easy, is possible only to minds with a high
degree of philosophical capacity.*' (Italics mine.) How is the 'degree
of philosophical capacity' measured?

§ 17. But we shall be accused of misrepresentation. 'You are neglecting', we shall be told, 'a vital distinction, which our theory emphasizes. What actually exists, what actually takes place, is always complex. The simple Qualities do not, as such, exist. They have being, or "are", eternally, timelessly, and not in place. Instances of them—actual cases or occurrences of them—are compounded of other elements besides their simple selves. What is actually being seen, exists and is a complex. The actual seeing occurs, and it too is a complex. Greenness in relation to this or these absolute points of Space, and that or those absolute moments of Time, is a complex which exists as a particular case of greenness : this green on that leaf here and now. Vision here and now, or then and there, is a complex fact, a particularized occurrence of the Simple Sentience which is related to the Simple Quality. We have insisted on this distinction, and we have described the peculiar relations of "occupying" Time and Space, which are involved.'

I confess that I have no acquaintance with 'absolute moments' and 'absolute points'. What an absolute moment or an absolute point may be, how it is distinguished from other absolute moments or points, how it is recognized, or how anything can be said about it which will serve to fix its absolute individuality : of all this I am ignorant, and I have not yet found any one to enlighten me. But for the sake of argument I will assume that there are such entities, and that the objector has an immediate and infallible acquaintance with some (if not with every one) of them. Still it seems to me that my criticism retains its force. For now it applies to the combination of the Atomic Simples, which constitute the existing complexes. That *these* Atomic Simples should combine to form a complex—or indeed that *any* Simples should combine—is a *de facto* coincidence, an arbitrary irrational fact, if it be 'a fact' at all. The objector himself is a mere unfounded coincidence : a 'class of psychical existents' related to certain absolute points of Space, and related also successively to certain absolute moments of Time.[1] And if I am told that facts are often irrational, and that these *de facto* coincidences *are* and must be accepted, still I must protest against the barbarous treatment to which the Simple Entities are subjected. How can you play fast and loose with their simplicity ? How can you treat them as each absolutely simple and independent, *and also* as related to one another to form a complex? *Greenness* here and now is *this* complex fact, this case of green actually existing. *The same greenness* there and then is *that* different complex fact, that case of green actually

---

[1] Cf. Russell, *Principles of Mathematics*, I, p. 523 : 'What we called, in chapter vi, the class as one, is an individual, provided its members are individuals : the objects of daily life, persons, tables, chairs, apples, &c., are classes as one. (A person is a class of psychical existents, the others are classes of material points, with perhaps some reference to secondary qualities.)' The addition of the temporal and spatial relations of the 'class of psychical existents' is suggested by what Mr. Russell says elsewhere (e.g. chap. liii): for a 'person' is related to a Body, and a Body is presumably a class of 'terms which occupy both points and instants'. But a 'class of psychical existents', with or without this addition, is an 'unfounded coincidence' in the sense of my criticism.

A somewhat different account of personal identity is tentatively propounded at p. 470 : 'Thus if the mind is anything, and if it can change, it must be something persistent and constant, to which all constituents of a psychical state have one and the same relation. Personal identity could be constituted by the persistence of this term, to which all a person's states (and nothing else) would have a fixed relation' . . . I regret that I cannot understand this passage. Is the 'persistent term' a simple entity within the personality, differing in its relation to the person from his other states solely by its persistence ? Or is this 'term'— as Mr. Russell's first sentence seems to say—identical with the whole mind? If so, are the 'constituents of a psychical state', the 'person's states', *not mental at all*, or, if mental, within *another* mind ?

existing. And again, neither here nor there, neither now nor then, *the same greenness* 'is' (we must not say 'exists'), pure and simple and self-contained, one of the ultimate components of the Universe. The temporal and spatial relations, I further understand you to say, are in all cases precisely and numerically *the same* relations. *The same greenness* is united, in the two cases, by two relations (each precisely and numerically *the same*) to a different pair of points and a different pair of moments. *The same greenness* and 'precisely and numerically the same' relations enter as constituents into an indefinite number of different complexes.[1]

[1] Cf. e.g. Russell, l.c., pp. 51, 52: 'I conclude, then, that the relation affirmed between A and B in the proposition "A differs from B" is the general relation of difference, and is precisely and numerically the same as the relation affirmed between C and D in "C differs from D". And this doctrine must be held, for the same reasons, to be true of all other relations: relations do not have instances, but are strictly the same in all propositions in which they occur.' I have assumed that the simple Qualities (like Relations) 'do not have instances': e.g. that the 'greenness' which is a constituent of *this* case of green is 'precisely and numerically the same' as the 'greenness' which is a constituent of *that* case of green, and also as 'greenness' pure and simple. *This* green and *that* green may be *called* 'numerically diverse instances' of the simple universal 'greenness'; but their numerical diversity (as I understand) is due to the different points and moments involved, and is not strictly a numerical difference in the 'greenness' which is a constituent of them. Mr. Russell, in a written reply which he has been good enough to send to me, repudiates the above interpretation of his doctrine. He says that his argument applies *only* to Relations; that on the question of 'particular greennesses' he has no opinion either way; and that he does not deny that 'greenness' *exists*. But if the simple Qualities (e.g. 'greenness') *exist*, the argument of §§ 15, 16 applies without any qualification, and I have no need to repeat it here. And the question whether 'greenness' *has* or *has not* numerically diverse instances of itself, is of no importance. For whichever alternative Mr. Russell may finally decide to adopt, his theory is equally impossible. If the simple 'greenness' becomes numerically multiple in the different complexes of which it forms a constituent, how can it be said to be 'unaffected' by being related to different entities? whilst, if it does *not* become numerically multiple, how can it—a simple numerically identical entity—enter into different existent complexes?

In this account of the union of Simple Entities to form Complexes, I can see nothing but a statement of the problem in terms which render its solution inconceivable. If you tell me that a penny in my pocket is 'the same' coin as a penny in yours, I agree that in a sense this is true enough. But if for the penny you substitute a simple eternal entity, and then go on to maintain that this simple self-identical entity is both in my pocket and in yours, and also in no place and at no time, I can only protest that a simplicity of this kind is too deep for me to fathom. Nor does it make the least difference if you *call* your simple entity a 'universal'. And if, finally, you insist that the relation of the simple entity to the points of Space which are *my* pocket, is *'precisely and numerically the same'* as its relation to the points of Space which are *your* pocket, I must admit that I am unable to distinguish a 'precise numerical identity' of this kind from numerical diversity.

If, on the other hand, each different complex involves different relations and different constituents, and each relation and each constituent is a simple entity, then (I suggest to you) the game is up. For then the Universe is really and unambiguously a multiplicity of Simples, and there is neither universality nor unity anywhere, except the unity of the units. Each Simple Element is what it professes to be, absolutely one, absolutely itself, absolutely other than everything else. And there, where your theory begins, it must also end. A Logic of abstract identity has carried you where it carried Antisthenes—beyond the reach of argument, and beyond the reach of knowledge.

For any monistic philosophy the fundamental difficulty is to find intelligible meaning within its system for the relative independence of the differences of the One. For any pluralistic philosophy the fundamental difficulty is to render any union of its ultimate simple entities intelligible without destroying their simplicity. In the first case we have One, and find it difficult to reconcile with its Unity the being of a variety or plurality within it. In the second case we have Many, and find it difficult, whilst retaining the simplicity and the independence of the elements of the Many, to recognize the being and the unity of anything not simple. With the difficulties of Monism I have here no special concern. I will only say that the Monist could 'solve' his difficulties with far fewer ultimate indefinables and immediate intuitions than the present pluralistic theory makes free to assume, though he would perhaps not call it a 'solution'. But what I here wish to point out is this: the present theory rests its account of the complex facts upon certain assumptions, which are simply and solely statements of the problem to be solved. Thus, it insists that the union of the Independent Simples is a union by external relations; and 'external relation' is a name for the problem to be solved. The problem is, 'How can elements, each absolutely simple and in itself, coalesce to form a complex in any sense a unity?' And the answer given is, 'By being externally related'; i. e. by coalescing to form a unity and yet *not* ceasing to be independent. Again, 'How can that, which is independent, yet be apprehended and known as independent?' The theory answers: 'In virtue of the *unique relation* of "experiencing" to the object experienced'; i.e. in virtue of an immediate apprehension which is just of the miraculous nature demanded for the solution of the problem. For this 'unique relation', when you ask what it is, is precisely the relation *which would have to characterize* an apprehension, if it apprehended its object and yet left that object independent. And finally, there is a problem as to how the simple, eternal, and self-identical can enter as a constituent into complexes, which are changing, different, and many. And the theory answers, 'By being related, in a not further explicable manner, to the different points and moments'. But these inexplicable relations are mere names for the problem. For they are simply formulations of the assertion that the simple, eternal, and self-identical is *yet also* a constituent of many different complexes, connected with many different places and times.[1]

§ 18. (2) I have endeavoured to show that the assumption that 'experiencing makes no difference to the facts' is either false, or irrelevant to the theory of truth which we are here discussing. And if my arguments have carried conviction, the remainder of my task will not be difficult. For it will not be hard to show that this theory, which set out to vindicate

---

[1] Hitherto I have assumed that the relation of 'experiencing' to the 'facts' is to be *external* in the sense that it is to leave *both relata* untouched and independent. Mr. Russell, however, in his article on 'Meinong's Theory', &c. (*Mind*, N.S., No. 52, p. 510), says: 'But the peculiarity of the cognitive relation . . . lies in this: that one term of the relation *is* nothing but an awareness of the other term—an awareness which may be either that of presentation or that of judgment. This makes the relation more essential, more intimate, than any other; for the relatedness seems to form part of the very nature of one of the related terms, namely of the psychical term.' I confess that this 'essential' and 'intimate' relation looks to me like a miracle postulated *ad hoc*, and a miracle strangely discordant with the philosophical position which it is designed to support. Mr. Russell's description of the cognitive relation appears to mean that, if A be the psychical term and B the other term, then A's very nature involves B, but B does not involve A. And although A's very nature involves B, it involves a B *in itself* or a B which is by its very nature *not* related to A or anything. For, given A, there is something, 'part of whose very nature' is 'relatedness': and relatedness presumably to something definite (viz. to *this* 'fact', B), not to a something in general which is nothing in particular. Yet although, given A, there is 'relatedness to B', the B in question must be *in itself* and *unrelated*; for otherwise what becomes of its 'independence'?

the independence of truth, must end by making truth
a private and personal possession, dependent upon an
individual intuition which itself is a particular psychical existent; unless indeed truth is to remain
entirely in itself, for ever unknown and unknowable
even to the advocates of the theory.[1] Truth is a
quality of certain propositions : it attaches to these
independent entities immediately and as they are in
themselves. Propositions *are* true or false, and their
truth or falsity have not to wait for our recognition.
Our recognition, when it comes, is—like the appreciation of a flavour—an immediate intuitive apprehension.
The truth as recognized, as known, is therefore a
matter of personal intuition—or rather of intuition
which is a psychical existent, one member of the
' class of psychical existents ' constituting a ' person '.[2]

'But', we shall be told, ' you are neglecting an
obvious distinction. For though the *recognition*, when
it comes, is intuitive, immediate, individual, and personal, the *truth in itself* is impersonal and independent.'

Truth *in itself*, truth neither known nor recognized,
may be anything you please. You can say what you
like about it, and it is not worth any one's while to
contradict you; for it remains beyond all and any
knowledge, and is a mere name for nothing. And I
hesitate to believe that the theory which we are criticizing worships this ' unknown God ', or maintains the
' independence of truth ' in this futile sense. The
truth, whose independence it wishes to vindicate, is
known or knowable, or in some way experienced.
' Yes', we shall be told, ' it is apprehended by an
immediate intuition, and in the intuition is recognized
as independent of the intuition.' But this is the old
assumption that ' experiencing makes no difference to
the facts ', interpreted in the sense in which it is false.

[1] Cf. above, p. 39.   [2] Cf. above. p. 46, note.

For let us consider once more what we are asked to accept. The truth as apprehended by the intuition is known, and known as independent. Independent *of what*? If the view means merely 'independent of the intuition *qua* this act of intuiting here and now', we may at once accept this with certain reservations. But if this were all that the view intended, the 'true', though not identical with the 'mental' *qua* this psychical occurrence, might still be essentially related to mind. Even an Idealist Logic would agree that truth is *in this sense* 'independent' of the intuition; but it would draw a distinction, which its critics do not appear to admit[1], between the intuition as apprehension of truth and the intuition as psychical fact, as this act of intuiting here and now. It would not agree that 'mind', or everything 'mental', is *nothing but* this psychical phenomenon, this psychical existent or class of psychical existents; nor would it admit without qualification that truth is *in no sense* 'here' or 'now', 'this' or 'that', but wholly and absolutely eternal, timeless, and unchanging. The theory sets on one side mind, everything mental or psychical; and on the other side the Simples (Qualities, Moments, and Points) and the Complexes or Propositions which are 'true' or 'false'. It interprets mind, the mental, as nothing but psychical fact or occurrence; and rightly refuses to identify the true with this. But since it recognizes nothing as mind or mental other than the mere psychical fact *qua* occurrence or *qua* existent, it is forced to identify the true with the non-mental, i. e. with that which is

---

[1] Cf. Russell, 'Meinong's Theory', &c. (I), *Mind*, N.S., No. 50, p. 204. '. . . that truth and falsehood apply not to beliefs, but to their objects; and that the object *of a thought*, even when this object does not exist, has a Being which is in no way dependent upon its being an object *of thought*: all these are theses which, though generally rejected, can be supported by arguments which deserve at least a refutation.' (Italics mine.)

independent of mind altogether, unknown and unknowable.[1] And it only appears to escape this conclusion by the postulate that 'experiencing makes no difference to the facts'; i.e. by assuming that in the purely factual and individual psychical occurrence 'the true' stands revealed in its universal, eternal, and independent nature. The true stands revealed in and to this psychical existent; but the revelation in no way affects the character of the existent psychical fact. That is, and remains, barely particular in spite of the universal character of what it apprehends; barely subjective, in spite of the independent being of the true which reveals itself to it; and a mere temporary occurrence, although it apprehends the timeless in its timelessness. The psychical existent may be an intuition of truth, 'belief in what is true' or knowledge'[2]; or it may be a perverted and illusory intuition, belief in what is false or 'error'. The difference falls entirely on the side of what is revealed. On the side of the mind there is in both cases alike a phenomenon of belief, which for the psychologist is *the same* fact. The content of the intuition, if it has a content, has nothing to do with truth or falsehood; for the content is psychical and is the concern of psychology, whilst truth and falsehood belong to the entirely extra-mental. They attach to the independent propositions, and are studied by the logician. The logician, however, is driven to the uncomfortable conception of a 'strictly logical assertion',

---

[1] Cf. e.g. Russell, *Principles of Mathematics*, I, p. 451: 'The argument that 2 is mental requires that 2 should be essentially an existent. But in that case it would be particular, and it would be impossible for 2 to be in two minds, or in one mind at two times. Thus 2 must be in any case an entity, which will have being even if it is in no mind.'

[2] Cf. Russell, l. c., *Mind*, N.S., No. 50, p. 205; No. 51, pp. 353, 354.

an assertion which is 'non-psychological'[1]; a conception which, if it means anything, is an attempt to reintroduce into the notion of truth essential relatedness to 'mind', and to restore to 'mind' its universal character. The psychologist is condemned to study mental states, psychical existents, in entire abstraction (if they are cognitional states) from *what* they apprehend or believe. And we have to introduce the science of Epistemology (more complex than Logic or Psychology, because it involves them both) to study knowledge. For knowledge *qua* 'belief' is the subject of Psychology, and *qua* belief in *what is true* presupposes the science of Logic.[2]

Now I would suggest to the advocates of this theory that there is an unpleasant choice before them, which they are bound to make.

(i) Are they prepared to abide by their pluralism? If so, the 'independent truth'—in the sense of the unknown and unknowable truth—may figure in their philosophy, if they think it worth while; but *the truth as known* will require a different consideration. For the truth as known will be the truth as revealed in and to *this* psychical existent. They may make their bow to the Independent Truth; but, except for this empty courtesy, their theory will be indistinguishable from extreme Subjective Idealism. Truth will be for them dependent upon the barely particular psychical existent, *my* belief or *your* belief.

(ii) Or do they prefer to abide by the independence of Truth *as known*? If so, let them develop to its consequences their conception of a 'logical assertion'; and let them examine their assumption that 'mind' and the 'mental' are nothing but particular occurrences or

---

[1] Above, p. 38.
[2] Above, p. 37. Cf. e.g. Russell, l. c., *Mind*, N.S., No. 50, p. 205.

existents. They will be driven to the recognition of a universal, which is neither a 'simple entity' nor a complex of simple constituents. They will begin to suspect their pluralism, and even perhaps to distrust the power of 'inexplicable relations' to constitute unity in a world of atomic simples.

§ 19. The only other alternative, so far as I can see, is to raise the old cry that 'experiencing makes no difference to the facts'; and to insist that my immediate intuition—*this* particular psychical existent—reveals to me the eternal independent truth, and reveals also to me that its revelation is of this kind.

I do not propose to bring forward any further arguments against this assumption; but I will add a few remarks on the meaning of 'immediate intuition'.

The bare fact that an apprehension is 'immediate' does not, to my mind, create a presumption in favour of its truth. On the contrary, it rouses suspicion. For an 'immediate apprehension' is one, the grounds of which are not stated; and if, in a philosophical treatise, the grounds of a belief are not stated, there is at least a possibility that the grounds are obscure, or perhaps even that there are no logical grounds. If, in a philosophical work, the author appeals to an immediate intuition, I inevitably suspect that his opinion rests on mere prejudice, or at least that he is unaware of its grounds. An 'immediate intuition', in short, is a belief which the believer cannot justify, or at any rate has not yet justified, by rational grounds. An 'immediate difference' is a difference vaguely apprehended; i. e. 'immediate difference' is the name given to an experience of difference which is as yet obscure and imperfectly developed, because the precise identity and the precise distinctions within the identity are not yet fully recognized. A difference which we accept, perhaps on rational but not yet explicit grounds, or perhaps without any logical justification (on 'psycho-logical grounds'), is accepted 'immediately'. And the immediacy, which attaches to our acceptance, is transferred to that which is experienced, and the experienced is called an 'immediate difference'. The difference e. g. between blue and red is for us at first *just* a difference. We feel it, experience it immediately, and there seems no more to be said. But as knowledge grows, we can and do mediate it. A *partial* mediation in the case just quoted is achieved, when we express the physical conditions of blue and red in terms of precise quantitative distinctions within the identity 'wave-lengths of ether'. Undoubtedly there remains in such cases, and perhaps in all cases, a residuum opaque to mediating thought. The Universe is one; but its unity is expressed and revealed in an infinity of individual differences, which retain for the finite mind their 'irrational flavour', their 'immediacy', however far the work of rational mediation has progressed. But the immediate apprehension of these individual differences sets its problems to thought, and is not their solution. And though thought cannot by its mediation exhaust the *data*—though finite intelligence cannot entirely overcome the opacity of its material—it attains to truth in so far as its mediation progresses, and not in so far as its progress is barred.

Everything which enters into human experience may 'be for' the experiencing subject in the form of immediacy, however inadequate that form may prove for some of the matter which comes under it. And because *every* experience may 'be for' the subject under this form, the 'immediacy' of an experience can as such decide neither its truth nor its falsity. That 'Baal is the only Lord,' that 'blue differs from red,' that '2 + 2 = 4', and that 'God was made man,' these are, or may be, all of them 'immediate experiences' and their 'immediacy' guarantees neither their truth nor their falsity. The fact that anything is experienced in the form of immediate feeling or intuition, or on the other hand in the form of mediate reflective thought, does not of itself approve the experience as true or condemn it as false. The truth or falsity of an experience depends, if you like to put it so, primarily upon *what* the experience is; but *what* the experience is, it is *as a whole*[1], and not in severance from the form under which its matter is experienced. And *what* 'the experience as a whole' is, can be revealed to human subjects only in so far as that experience is raised to the level of mediate thought. It is in the attempt to mediate our 'immediate experiences' that their truth or falsity is revealed; and except in so far as that attempt is made, and in being made succeeds or fails, they possess for us neither truth nor falsity.

Thus 'blue differs from red', and '$2 + 2 = 4$'; and these 'immediate experiences' are said to be true. But their truth is revealed to us only in so far as they endure the test of mediation. Their 'truth' means for us that a whole system of knowledge stands and falls with them, and that in that system they survive[2] as necessary constituent elements. Again, the believer's intuition that 'Baal is the only Lord' is an immediate experience, which is false. But if it be false, its falsity does not depend upon its immediacy. It is not *because* it is an emotional unmediated faith that it is false, any more than the Christian's emotional

---

[1] If we are to sever the form of apprehending from the matter apprehended, we must look rather to the matter than to the form as determining the truth or falsity of the total experience. But the severance, I should contend, is indefensible; and, if it is made, the problem as to the nature of truth and falsity will remain insoluble.

[2] See below, §§ 30-7.

faith that 'God was made man' is true (if it be true) *because* of its immediacy. That the 'immediate experience' of the Baal-worshipper is false, means for us in the end that it will not stand mediation. The moral and religious experiences of the past and the present (even of the Baal-worshippers themselves) reveal themselves, when critically analysed and reconstructed, as a texture into which *this* immediate intuition can in no sense be woven; they form a system in which *this* would-be truth cannot as such survive.

No doubt there are 'immediate experiences' which have left mediation behind, and which sum up in themselves, in a clarified and concentrated form, the work of critical analysis and reflective reconstruction. The 'beatific vision' of the saint, the 'inspiration' of the artist, the 'intuition' of the scientific discoverer, are all of them 'immediate experiences'. And, sometimes at any rate, they indicate a level of consciousness more developed (and not more inchoate) than the level of the discursive understanding. But even so it is not *qua* 'immediate' that such experiences command the respect of the seeker after truth. Their claim to be experiences of the truth is entitled to recognition only in so far as their transparent form of immediate intuition is the outcome and the sublimated expression of rational mediation. Otherwise they are legitimate objects of suspicion and distrust.

§ 20. We have rejected the view that Truth and Falsity are qualities of independent entities, immediate flavours, so to say, of 'propositions' which are by no means 'mental' or essentially related to mind. We have refused to admit that 'experiencing makes no difference to the facts,' in the sense that 'the facts' are what they are in and for themselves, and in entire independence of any and all experience of them. Experience, we have insisted, is a unity of two factors essentially inter-related and reciprocally involving each other for their being and their nature. Truth and Falsity do not attach to one of those factors *in itself*, if only for the reason that neither factor is, or can be, *in itself*.

With this conclusion we might be content to pass on. But, before we do so, it will be best to guard ourselves against a misunderstanding, which is possible and indeed probable, though not really justified by what we have said. For we may be told, that if our opponents have erred by abstraction, we ourselves are equally guilty. We have denied that Truth and Falsity attach to propositions in themselves, for we have denied that Qualities and Propositions in themselves ' are ' anything but unreal abstractions. It may be assumed that *therefore* we are bound to maintain that Truth and Falsity attach to the psychical occurrences, or states, of *this* and *that* finite individual *as such*; and that what ' is ', and what *alone* ' is ', is the finite subject and his psychical events. In short, it may be assumed that, since we have rejected a Realistic Pluralism, we must be advocating a Subjective Idealism; and that, having insisted that ' experiencing makes a difference to the facts ', we must mean that *this* or *that* psychical occurrence, *this* factual event in or of *my* mind, constitutes and is the only Reality and the only Truth.

It will not help us to protest that *my mind* (as an independent, purely self-contained and exclusive, entity) and *my ideas* (as mere psychical existents) are unreal abstractions, which we have done our best to discredit.[1] ' For surely,' it will be said, ' *my* mind is at any rate not *yours*, and at any rate it occurs in time with its own individual and distinctive process. A

[1] Cf. above, pp. 24, 25.

mind in general is a fiction as unreasonable as a psychical state which is not particularized in time, and
not confined to an individual subject. And how
would it help you, even if we admitted this universal
mind, which is neither *mine* nor *yours*, whose processes
and states are not existent and particular, but timeless
and universal? It would be a mind whose thoughts
might be "true", but its thoughts would have no
relation to our thoughts, and their "truth" would be
in a world apart from human judgement and inference. Moreover, though you disclaim the title of
Subjective Idealists, you call yourselves Idealists;
and Idealism is and must be Subjective Idealism.
Out of its own mouth it stands condemned. For,
though it may make play with a distinction between
two factors within experience—that which is experienced and the experiencing thereof—it is ultimately
driven to recognize *mind and nothing but mind* everywhere. In the end it is forced to maintain that whatever *is* is "spirit" or "spiritual", "mind" or "mental", a "self" or "psychical states and processes" of
a "self". Knowledge is for it that process in which
mind comes to recognition of itself; that consummation in which "spirit greets spirit", or in which the
objectivity and externality in the subject-matter vanish
into the "transparent subjectivity" of pure self-consciousness, i.e. of "thought thinking thought". Reality, for all forms of Idealism, is of this "unsubstantial stuff". It is "ideas", "thoughts", "spiritual"
or "psychical" processes; and these and their like *are*
in, or of, individual minds. If, then, you face the
logical consequences of your idealistic position, the
Universe will be for you the complex of the psychical
processes within a finite spirit, viz. yourself. Such
a complex, invested perhaps with the kind of inner
consistency which attaches to a coherent dream, is the

utmost that you are logically entitled to accept as Real. For there is no logical warrant for the ornamental additions which some Idealists have made to their Solipsism. They have no right to recognize other finite spirits or a divine and infinite spirit, except as psychical states of their own, as part and parcel of their dream.'

Subjective Idealism has rightly fallen into discredit. It will not stand as a theory of Reality; and it affords no foundation for a sane theory of knowledge or of conduct. It fails when it takes the consistent form of Solipsism; and it fails equally when it assumes the half-hearted form of a spiritual pluralism. Neither I myself and my psychical states, nor an assemblage of finite selves each wrapped up in his own ideas, can constitute the ultimate reality. And the failure of Subjective Idealism is in no way lessened by the introduction of an infinite mind and its psychical states *besides* the finite self or selves. It is indeed ' a short way with Idealists ' to identify them with the advocates of this type of theory : and if the identification were established, Idealism would be finally refuted.[1] But the point at issue is whether this

---

[1] Cf. G. E. Moore, 'The Refutation of Idealism,' *Mind*, N.S., No. 48, pp. 433–53. The reader of Mr. Moore's article will notice that he has made his task easy for himself by his formulation of the purport of Idealism. Cf. e.g. p. 433 : 'Modern Idealism, if it asserts any general conclusion about the universe at all, asserts that it is *spiritual*. . . Chairs and tables and mountains *seem* to be very different from us ; but, when the whole universe is declared to be spiritual, it is certainly meant to assert that they are far more like us than we think. The idealist means to assert that they are *in some sense* neither lifeless nor unconscious, as they certainly seem to be ; and I do not think his language is so grossly deceptive, but that we may assume him to believe that they really are very different indeed from what they seem.' On p. 434 'stars' and 'planets', 'cups' and 'saucers', take the place of 'chairs and tables and mountains' as examples of things which the Idealist is supposed to regard as being 'really very different indeed from what they seem'. When Spinoza maintained that 'omnia, quamvis

identification is sound or not : and I am contending
that it is not. The Subjective Idealist maintains that
he knows directly only his own ideas or psychical
states, is aware only of affections of his psychical
subjectivity. He is confined to states and processes of
his own self-contained and exclusive psychical being.
Anything else—if there be anything else—is *for him*, as
he knows it, a state or process of himself. And if, by
a precarious inference or by an illogical postulate, he
admits the being of other finite subjects and of an
infinite subject or God, these are all external to one
another and to him, and self-contained and exclusive
like himself. But throughout I have been insisting
that self-contained and exclusive entities of this kind
are fictions. I have tried to show that the Universe
is not a whole of independent and reciprocally-exclusive
parts, and that a Universal is not another entity along-
side of its particulars. It is unwarrantable, therefore,
to accuse me of postulating a 'universal mind which
is neither mine nor yours', or a 'mind in general', or
a 'divine mind' which is external to the finite minds.
Such a postulate is utterly inconsistent with all that
we have been maintaining ; and certainly it would in
no way support our theory. And if, in the consum-

diversis gradibus, animata tamen sunt', some critics were naïve
enough to protest that a stone or a lamp or a chair surely had no
soul. Similarly, Mr. Moore appears to suppose that the Idealists,
who hold that the universe is in its ultimate reality 'spiritual',
understand by *the universe in its ultimate reality* the assemblage of
what the unreflecting perceptive consciousness takes as 'things'.
Chairs, tables, mountains, stars, planets, cups and saucers, Mr.
Moore apparently assumes, *are as such ultimately real*. Ordinary
people attach certain properties to them ; and then the Idealist,
with his strange love of paradox, attaches quite other properties
to them. They—the chairs and tables and saucers, &c.—remain
these individual things ; but have now 'in some sense' acquired
life and consciousness. Even if Mr. Moore really had reduced all
Idealism to Subjective Idealism, his 'refutation' is far from convincing ; but it will be time enough for Idealists to meet Mr.
Moore's 'refutation' when the reduction has been made.

mation of knowledge, 'spirit greets spirit', or 'mind recognizes itself', or self-consciousness has become 'the transparent unity of thought with thought for its object', has any Idealist ever suggested that this consummation is embodied e. g. in *my apprehension of this green leaf here and now*, taken strictly and solely as *this my particular experience*? Or has any Idealist acquiesced in the interpretation which identifies 'spirit', 'mind', 'consciousness'—the 'spiritual', the 'mental'—with purely particular, self-contained, exclusive existents capable of *external* (and no other) relations to one another?

CHAPTER III

TRUTH AS COHERENCE

(i) THE COHERENCE-NOTION OF TRUTH

§ 21. OUR inquiry into the nature of truth has not so far been rewarded with conspicuous success. We have examined two types of theory, and both have crumbled away before our criticism. The essential nature of truth does not lie in the correspondence of knowledge with reality. Truth is not adequately conceived as the ideal representation of fact, or as the image which faithfully reflects an original. And, again, truth is not a quality, an immediate characteristic flavour, of independent entities which are what they are in and for themselves without relation to mind.

Of these negative results we have convinced ourselves, even if we have failed to convince the reader. Incidentally, moreover, our discussion has led us to reject yet another view. No special virtue attaches to immediate apprehension: and the truth is not essentially and in its nature 'immediate', even though it may sometimes be manifested in an intuitive or immediate form. What is true, is true not *because* but *in spite of* the immediacy of the experience in which it is sometimes revealed.

Our results are thus in appearance purely negative. We seem to have destroyed everything, even the materials for a possible reconstruction. But a more careful consideration will show that we have in reality made some progress towards a more adequate conception of truth. For our criticism was developed under the control of a positive notion of truth. How other-

wise, indeed, could our criticism convince us that itself
was true? And this positive notion, from which our
criticism drew its destructive power, came to the
surface in the course of our discussion. Its main
features, its characteristic if somewhat shadowy outline, emerged as that *other* view of truth on which we
found ourselves driven back: the view of truth as
'systematic coherence'.[1] It may be difficult, but it
is surely not impossible, to develop these fragmentary
indications into a full and definite exposition of the
coherence-notion of truth.

If we succeed in formulating this theory, we must
then examine it as we have examined the others;
but we may approach our task with an assurance
which should give us comfort. For the coherence-
theory, even though it may fail to run the gauntlet of
all criticism, at least goes deeper than the theories we
have rejected. It is not simply another theory on the
same level, side by side with them. It is the source
from which they draw what speculative value they
possess. So far as their attractions are not merely
meretricious, they attract by masquerading in its
finery. It has emerged in our discussion—so far as
it *has* emerged—as the substantial basis underlying
their perverted and perverse expressions. Hence we
may rest confidently in our critical rejection of them.
We have tested them and found them wanting; and
this verdict we need never recall. Doubtless our
criticism of them implied the coherence-notion of
truth; and doubtless that notion may prove neither
ultimate nor complete. Yet most certainly it is more
complete and more nearly ultimate than the rejected
theories; and if we are obliged in the end to reject it,
our rejection will not reinstate the earlier views, but
only confirm our condemnation of them.

[1] Cf. above, pp. 16, 17, 22, 23, 28, 42 note, 56–8.

§ 22. We may start with the following as a
provisional and rough formulation of the coherence-
notion. 'Anything is true which can be conceived.
It is true because, and in so far as, it can be conceived. Conceivability is the essential nature of
truth'. And we may proceed at once to remove
a possible misunderstanding of the term 'conceive'.
We do not mean by 'conceive' to form a mental
picture ; and we shall not be dismayed when we
hear that the Antipodes were once 'inconceivable',
or that a Centaur can be 'conceived'. For it may be
difficult—or even, if you like, impossible—to 'image'
people walking head downwards ; and to 'picture'
a horse with the head and shoulders of a man may
be as easy as you please. All this is quite irrelevant,
and does not touch our position. To 'conceive'
means for us to think out clearly and logically, to hold
many elements together in a connexion necessitated
by their several contents. And to be 'conceivable'
means to be a 'significant whole', or a whole possessed
of meaning for thought. A 'significant whole' is
such that all its constituent elements reciprocally
involve one another, or reciprocally determine one
another's being as contributory features in a single
concrete meaning. The elements thus cohering constitute a whole which may be said to control the
reciprocal adjustment of its elements, as an end
controls its constituent means. And in this sense
a Centaur is 'inconceivable', whilst the Antipodes
are clearly 'conceivable'. For the elements constitutive of the Centaur refuse to enter into reciprocal
adjustment. They collide amongst themselves, or
they clash with some of the constitutive elements in
that wider sphere of experience, that larger significant
whole, in which the Centaur must strive for a place.
The horse-man might pass externally as a convenient

shape for rapid movement; but how about his internal
economy, the structure, adjustment and functioning of
his inner organs? If he is to be ' actual ', the animal
kingdom is his natural home. But if we persisted in
our attempt to locate the creature there, we should
inevitably bring confusion and contradiction into that
sphere of significant being—so far at least as it is
manifest to us in our anatomical and physiological
knowledge. And, on the other hand, the being of
the Antipodes is a necessary interconnected piece in
that puzzle of which our astronomical science is the
coherent exposition. The Antipodes are 'conceivable'
in the sense that they are *forced* upon any thinker for
whom the earth and the solar system are to possess
significance; i. e. the Antipodes are a necessary constituent of a significant whole, as that whole must be
conceived.[1]

§ 23. Thus ' conceivability' means for us *systematic*

---

[1] I have not referred to the negative formulation, which finds
the criterion of a necessary truth in the inconceivability of its
opposite. Is it true e.g. that the diagonal of a square is incommensurate with its side? Try whether its commensurability is
conceivable. If it be inconceivable, the original thesis is established as a ' necessary' truth. Such a view was attributed to
Whewell by Mill (*Logic*, II, ch. v, § 6), in his controversy as to the
ground of our belief in the mathematical axioms. But the distinction between 'necessary' and 'contingent' truths is not one
which I should be prepared to accept; and, even apart from that,
the negative formulation is unsuitable for our present purpose. A
criterion of truth—i.e. something other than the truth itself, by
which we are to recognize the truth—is not what we require. We
want to know what truth in its nature is, not by what characteristics in its opposing falsehood we may infer its presence. Yet it
is only the latter purpose which is facilitated by the roundabout
method through the inconceivability of the opposite. The opposite
is sometimes more accessible to our experiments: it is easier to
try (and to fail) to conceive the false, than to try with success
to conceive the true. But this is a mere psychological fact—an
accident of our convenience—and does not enter into the constitution of truth as an essential element of its nature. The baffled
attempt, in other words, is at best a *causa cognoscendi* of the
truth, not its *causa essendi*.

coherence, and is the determining characteristic of a 'significant whole'. The systematic coherence of such a whole is expressed most adequately and explicitly in the system of reasoned knowledge which we call a science or a branch of philosophy.[1] Any element of such a whole shares in this characteristic to a greater or less degree—i. e. is more or less 'conceivable'—in proportion as the whole, with its determinate inner articulation, shines more or less clearly through that element; or in proportion as the element, in manifesting itself, manifests also with more or less clearness and fullness the remaining elements in their reciprocal adjustment.

It is obvious that this rough sketch suggests many difficult problems. Truth, we have said, *is* in its essence conceivability or systematic coherence; and now we seem to have severed 'the conceivable' from its expression, the 'significant whole' from the forms in which its significance is revealed. The truth, therefore, would apparently fall on the side of the Real; and would stand over against science or reasoned knowledge, faith, emotion, volition, &c., as the various subjective modes in which it obtains actuality and

[1] I am not denying that a 'significant whole' may find expression in other forms and at other levels than that of discursive thinking. The moral ideal e.g. is a significant whole, which finds expression in the ordered life of a people, in their maintenance of the laws and institutions, in their reasonable but unreflective habitual conduct, in their conscience, sense of duty and justice, love of country, love of family and friends, &c., &c. But this significant whole *in its character as truth* is most adequately expressed at the level of reflective thinking, and in the form of the science or philosophy of conduct; for such a science is the explicit analysis and the reasoned reconstruction of the inner organization (the systematic coherence) of the moral ideal. Similarly, aesthetic and religious ideals are significant wholes; and their systematic coherence or truth is most adequately revealed in the reflective form of a philosophy of art or of religion. Yet they also use the emotion of the artist and art-lover, or the faith of the devout but unthinking worshipper, as more immediate vehicles of their actuality.

recognition. But this severance of the experienced Real from the experiencing of it, is the very mistake against which the main discussions of our second chapter were directed; whilst, if truth be thus located in a sphere of being apart from mind, it is difficult to see how science can in any sense be 'true'. We spoke of science as an explicit analysis and reasoned reconstruction of the systematic coherence of a significant whole; but this sounds uncommonly like a reversion to the correspondence-notion. Science would be 'true', so far as its system of demonstrations reconstructs—i. e. *repeats or corresponds to*—the systematic coherence which *is* the truth as a character of the Real.

Moreover, we have admitted degrees of conceivability, and therefore also degrees of truth. But we have not explained, and perhaps could not explain, the ideal of perfect conceivability and perfect truth by reference to which these degrees are to be estimated.

Before I turn to the consideration of these problems, let me endeavour to throw further light on the theory just sketched, by contrasting it with two very different views to which it bears some superficial resemblance. The time and labour occupied in this comparison will not be wasted; for it will enable us to develop a more adequate formulation of the coherence-notion, and we shall approach the problems to be solved with a more just appreciation of their precise difficulty.

§ 24. (i) When Descartes laid it down as a principle for the seeker after truth 'to affirm nothing as true except that which he could clearly and distinctly perceive', he was in reality presupposing a very definite theory of knowledge and a correspondingly determinate metaphysics [1]. If we wish to pass a true judgement,

---

[1] Descartes' full meaning is best seen by comparing his *Regulae ad directionem ingenii* with the corresponding passages in the *Discours de la Méthode*, the *Meditationes*, and the *Principia Philoso-*

we must affirm or deny only that content which we
clearly and distinctly apprehend. Inner affirmation,
or denial, which is the characteristic of judgement,
is an act in which we exhibit our free choice or
will.[1] But this act is exercised upon a material in the
acceptance of which we are passive. The intellect—
a passive recipient—apprehends a content, which the
will—an active faculty—may affirm or deny. And
if this affirmation is to constitute a true judgement,
the content affirmed must force itself upon our
intellect as a self-evident *datum*, which we immediately
recognize as indubitable. Thus the immediate apprehension of indubitable truth, an ' intuition ', is the
necessary pre-condition of truth of judgement.[2] The
content of such an ' intuition ', viz. that which we
apprehend intuitively as self-evident, is a ' simple
idea ', or rather (as Descartes sometimes [3] more clearly
expresses it) a ' simple proposition '. Its ' simplicity '
does not exclude inner distinction ; for it is the imme-

phiae. On the whole subject cf. Adamson, *The Development of
Modern Philosophy*, Vol. I, ch. i, and Broder Christiansen, *Das
Urteil bei Descartes.*

[1] In certain cases we exhibit our freedom by neither affirming
nor denying, but by suspending our will. But this is a detail of
the theory which we can here disregard.—The affirmation (or
negation) involved in judgement is *internal* ; cf. e.g. Descartes'
answer to Hobbes: 'Per se notum est . . . aliud esse videre hominem
currentem, quam sibi ipsi affirmare se illum videre, quod fit sine
voce.' (*Obi. et Resp. tertiae,* answer to objection vi).

[2] This double and ambiguous use of ' truth '—truth of judgement
and truth of apprehension—exposes Descartes' theory of knowledge to serious criticism. But I cannot enter into the matter
here. Neither is this the place to discuss the ambiguity in
Descartes' statements concerning the ' Intellect ' and ' Ideas '. At
times ' ideas ' are simply modes, phases, determinate states of the
intellect ; but at other times the intellect is said to ' attend to '
ideas, which it ' finds ' in itself. Cf. and contrast *Notae in progr.
quodd.* (pp. 158 and 163 in the edition of 1692), Letter of 1644
(Adam & Tannery, IV, 113) and *Regulae* i, xii, *Medit.* vi. On
the whole subject, cf. Norman Smith, *Studies in the Cartesian
Philosophy*, p. 52, pp. 90 ff.

[3] Particularly in the *Regulae* ; cf. e.g. *Reg.* iii, xi, xii.

diate, but necessary, cohesion of two elements or two constituent ideas. In other words, the self-evident *datum*, which Descartes calls a 'simple idea' or a 'simple proposition', is a hypothetical judgement so formulated that the antecedent immediately necessitates the consequent, though the consequent need not reciprocally involve the antecedent.[1]

The elements in the content of an 'intuition' cohere by the immediate necessity which binds consequent to antecedent in a hypothetical judgement of the kind explained. But the content *as a whole* is grasped intuitively, or immediately, as an indubitable self-evident *datum*. Such self-evident indubitable truths constitute the foundation on which the structure of scientific and philosophical knowledge is built. They are the principles, from which the whole system of demonstrated and demonstrable truth must be derived.[2]

[1] Cf. Descartes' own instances : 'cogito ergo sum', i.e. 'if self-consciousness, then existence', but not necessarily also 'if existence, then self-consciousness'. So '$2+2=4$', i.e. 'if 2 be added to 2, there must be 4'; but there may be 4 without this mode of addition, as is evident from '$3+1=4$', which Descartes quotes as another instance of 'Intuition'. Cf. *Regulae*, iii; and, on the whole subject, see Adamson, l. c. p. 10, note 3 ; and Christiansen, l. c. pp. 28 ff.

[2] The mediate truths are reached from the immediate self-evidents by a process which Descartes calls 'deduction'. The logical character of this process is *not* syllogistic (cf. e.g. *Regulae*, x). It is a pure illation of the mind, which, in the simplest cases, is hardly distinguishable from the immediate intuition of a necessary nexus within a content. Thus e.g. we intuite that $2+2=4$, and again that $3+1=4$; we *deduce* that $3+1=2+2$. But the latter (mediate) truth, when the movement of the mind is over, is itself grasped immediately, i.e. becomes an 'intuition' (cf. e.g. *Regulae*, iii, xi). In such cases, the term 'deduction' marks the movement of illation in distinction from the concentrated grasp of the articulated content in which that movement culminates and rests. In more complex cases, the inference presupposes an ordered grouping of the many self-evidents, from which the grasp of the mediate truth is ultimately to emerge. To this preparatory grouping Descartes gives the name of *induction* or *enumeration* ; and he occasionally extends

And this system is, so to say, a network of chains of propositions. The links in each chain form an uninterrupted sequence from its first link. They follow with unbroken logical coherence from a self-evident *datum*, a 'simple proposition' apprehended intuitively. Each derivative link is grasped by the intellect as the necessary consequent of a link or links intuited as indubitable truths, and *as thus grasped* itself is manifest as an indubitable truth.

Thus, the ideal of knowledge for Descartes is a coherent system of truths, where each truth is apprehended in its logical position: the immediate as the basis, and the mediate truths in their necessary dependence on the immediate. Each truth in this ideal system is a cohesion of different elements united by a logical nexus; and every truth is true *per se* absolutely and unalterably.

But the theory which I am trying to expound is committed, for good or for evil, to a radically different view of the systematization of knowledge. The image of a chain, admirably suited to illustrate the theory of Descartes, is a sheer distortion of the conception of 'coherence' or 'conceivability', which, on my view, characterizes truth. The ideal of knowledge for me is a system, not of *truths*, but of *truth*. 'Coherence' cannot be attached to propositions from the outside:

these titles to the inference as a whole (cf. *Regulae*, vii, xi, xii). But even here the logical character of the inference remains the same. The 'deduction', 'induction,' or 'enumeration', is always the illative movement from a content or contents intuitively apprehended to another content which follows by direct logical necessity from the first. And it is a mere accident, due e.g. to the limitations of our memory, that the movement does not always issue in an 'intuition'. I cannot enter into further details here, though I am aware that *inductio* (or *enumeratio*) is usually interpreted as a distinct method of proof, differing in logical character from *deductio*. But I believe that a careful study of the *Regulae* will convince the reader that my interpretation is essentially correct, however paradoxical it may appear.

it is not a property which they can acquire by colliga-
tion, whilst retaining unaltered the truth they possessed
in isolation. And whereas for Descartes ideally certain
knowledge (indubitable truth) is typified in the intuitive grasp of the immediately cohering elements of
a 'simple proposition', such a content is for me so
remote from the ideal as hardly to deserve the name
of 'truth' at all. For it is the smallest and most
abstracted fragment of knowledge, a mere mutilated
shred torn from the living whole in which alone it
possessed its significance. The typical embodiments
of the ideal must be sought, not in such isolated intuitions, but rather in the organized whole of a science:
for that possesses at least *relative* self-dependence, and
its significance is at least *relatively* immanent and self-
contained.

§ 25. (ii) The second view with which I propose to
contrast the coherence-theory may be regarded as
a corollary of the first.[1] For, if there are certain
judgements indubitably true, then these are the
materials of knowledge. And, in the progress of
thought, a *form* is imposed upon these materials which
arranges without altering them. Truth is linked to
truth until the arrangement constitutes that network
of chains of truths which is the system of ideally
complete knowledge. The form under which the
infinitely various materials are ordered, is the universal form of all thinking. It is the characteristic grey
of formal consistency, which any and every thinking
monotonously paints over all its materials to stamp
them as its own. This arrangement under the form
of thinking cannot *of itself* guarantee the truth of the
result. For false materials, as well as true, may be
painted with the royal colour. But the result cannot

[1] I do not suggest that the two views were *historically* so
related.

be true *without* this arrangement, which is thus a *sine qua non* or a 'negative condition' of truth. We may christen the observance of this condition 'validity'; and we may then draw the conclusion that the completely true must also be valid, though the valid may be false. Or if we prefer the term 'consistency' we shall point out that consistent lying and consistent error are occasionally achieved, and that a man may be a consistent scoundrel; but that the truth requires for its apprehension and utterance the same consistency of thought and purpose, which must also be expressed in the actions of the morally good man. The consistent, in short, need be neither true nor good; but the good and the true must be consistent.

This distinction between the universal form and the particular materials of thought has, in various modifications, played a great part in the history of philosophy. I am here concerned with it in its barest and most extreme shape, as the fundamental assumption of the traditional 'formal' logic. Pressed beyond the limits of legitimate provisional abstraction until it has become a mere caricature, the antithesis between form and matter has in that 'science'[1] been worked out through the whole domain and through all the functions of thinking. Judgement e. g. is that function of thought whereby two conceptions are combined; and whatever the materials, the form of combination exhibits a character of its own, which is to be studied apart. Hence those classifications of 'formal' logic which we have all of us learnt, and learnt to unlearn again: those rigid groupings of Judgements as Universal, Individual, Particular; as Negative, Affirmative, Infinite; as Categorical, Hypothetical, Necessary, &c., &c. So, Syllogism is the function of thought whereby

---

[1] Or 'art': it does not matter which title we give to what is neither one nor the other.

two judgements are combined to generate a third; and 'formal' logic gives you the rules of 'valid' combination irrespective of *what* is combined, and impotent therefore to determine the truth of the result.

Formal logic, in this sense of the term, might be called 'the analysis of low-grade thinking'[1]; but all thinking, even at its lowest, is a living process, which the mechanical methods of such an analysis are too crude to grasp. Yet all thinking—the most complicated and profound, as well as the most shallow and rudimentary—exhibits a certain unity of character. And the formal logician has followed a sound instinct in emphasizing the necessity of analysing and grasping this unity, if thinking is to understand itself. But he has erred in looking for the unity as an abstract common feature, to be found in the actual processes of thinking by stripping them of their concrete differences. And it is the same error which has led him to conceive thinking as a dead and finished product instead of a living and moving process. In the end and in principle his error is the failure to conceive a universal except as one element along with others in the particular: a failure which is tantamount to the negation of all universals. Or it is the failure to conceive a whole except as the sum of its parts: a failure which is the denial of unity and individual character to that which develops and lives. Hence formal logic assumes that the essential nature of thought is to be found in an abstractly self-identical form; in a tautologous self-consistency, where the 'self' has no diversity of content in which a genuine consistency could be manifested, or where diversity of content is cast aside as mere irrelevant material. But the essential nature of thought is a concrete unity, a living individuality. Thought is a form, which moves and expands, and

[1] Cf. e.g. Bosanquet, *Knowledge and Reality*, 2nd issue, p. 193.

exhibits its consistent character precisely in those ordered articulations of its structure which formal logic impotently dismisses as *mere* materials.

The 'systematic coherence', therefore, in which we are looking for the nature of truth, must not be confused with the 'consistency' of formal logic. A piece of thinking might be free from self-contradiction, might be 'consistent' and 'valid' as the formal logician understands those terms, and yet it might fail to exhibit that systematic coherence which is truth.

§ 26. We may now proceed to formulate the coherence-theory afresh in the following terms. Truth in its essential nature is that systematic coherence which is the character of a significant whole. A 'significant whole' is an organized individual experience, self-fulfilling and self-fulfilled. Its organization *is* the process of its self-fulfilment, and the concrete manifestation of its individuality. But this process is no mere surface-play between static parts within the whole: nor *is* the individuality of the whole, except in the movement which is its manifestation. The whole *is* not, if 'is' implies that its nature is a finished product prior or posterior to the process, or in any sense apart from it. And the whole *has* no parts, if 'to have parts' means to consist of fixed and determinate constituents, from and to which the actions and interactions of its organic life proceed, much as a train may travel backwards and forwards between the terminal stations. Its 'parts' are through and through in the process and constituted by it. They are 'moments' in the self-fulfilling process which is the individuality of the whole. And the individuality of the whole is *both* the pre-supposition of the distinctive being of its 'moments' or parts *and* the resultant which emerges as their co-operation, or which they make and continuously sustain.

It is this process of self-fulfilment which is truth, and it is *this* which the theory means by 'systematic coherence'. The process is not a movement playing between static elements, but the very substance of the moving elements. And the coherence is no abstract form imposed upon the surface of materials, which retain in their depths a nature untouched by the imposition. The coherence—if we call it a 'form'—is a form which through and through inter-penetrates its materials; and they—if we call them 'materials'—are materials, which retain no inner privacy for themselves in independence of the form. They hold their distinctive being in and through, and not in sheer defiance of, their identical form; and its identity is the concrete sameness of different materials. The materials *are* only as moments in the process which is the continuous emergence of the coherence. And the form *is* only as the sustained process of self-fulfilment, wherein just these materials reveal themselves as constitutive moments of the coherence.

In the above formulation I have endeavoured to express the coherence-notion so as to emphasize the *concreteness* of the coherence which is truth, as against the view which found truth in formal consistency [1]; and I have insisted upon the conception of truth as a living and moving whole, as against the Cartesian view of fixed truths on which the structure of knowledge is built. [2] But the result at present is a mere vague sketch, which cannot pretend to be satisfactory. Even the well-disposed reader will regard it as the description of a mystical ideal with no obvious application to the actual problems of human knowledge; whilst the hostile critic will view it as a dishonest evasion of the difficulties, as mere words in place of a solid discussion. I shall accordingly

[1] Cf. above, § 25.　　　　　　　[2] Cf. above, § 24.

attempt to work out my sketch in detail, so as to show the precise bearing of this conception of truth on the truth in human judgement and inference, and so as to defend it against the charge of mysticism or evasion of the difficulties.

§ 27. If we are to develop our vague sketch into a definite theory, we must make it clear *what* truth we are professing to describe. Was our sketch intended as an exposition of truth as it is for human knowledge? or were we describing an ideal experience, which no finite mind can ever actually enjoy?

This manner of formulating the question seems to challenge a choice between two unambiguous alternatives, and thus to put a clear issue before us. But in reality it involves certain assumptions which are open to debate, and which—as I think, and hope to show—are false.[1] For it is assumed that finite experience is sundered by a gulf from ideal experience. It is implied that an ideal experience is as such debarred from actuality, and it is suggested that knowledge which is severed from ideal experience can yet be true. But, whilst refusing to commit myself to these implications, I should reply that my sketch was intended to describe the nature of truth as an ideal, as the character of an ideally complete experience. Truth, we said, was the systematic coherence which characterized a significant whole. And we proceeded to identify a significant whole with 'an organized individual experience, self-fulfilling and self-fulfilled'. Now there can be one *and only one* such experience: or *only one* significant whole, the significance of which is self-contained in the sense required. For it is *absolute* self-fulfilment, *absolutely* self-contained significance, that is postulated; and nothing short of *absolute*

[1] Cf. below, pp. 82, 83.

individuality—nothing short of *the* completely whole experience—can satisfy this postulate. And human knowledge—not merely *my* knowledge or *yours*, but the best and fullest knowledge in the world at any stage of its development—is clearly not a significant whole in this ideally complete sense. Hence the truth, which our sketch described, is—*from the point of view of the human intelligence*—an Ideal, and an Ideal which can never *as such*, or in its completeness, be actual as human experience.

But it will be contended that such an Ideal cannot be expressed in terms of human thought, and is strictly inconceivable. 'All attempts to conceive your Ideal', we shall be told, 'are foredoomed to failure. For we cannot conceive, except under categories whose meaning is moulded and restricted by the limitations of that finite experience in which alone they have any legitimate application. We employ categories with a determinate meaning in their application to the incomplete experience, which is actually ours : but their meaning is determinate, only in so far as it is relative to the area in which the restricting conditions hold. Yet the conception of your Ideal requires the absolute and unrestricted use of these categories. But, if they are used absolutely, we can conceive nothing determinate under them : we are playing with empty words. Whilst, if they are used under the restrictions which condition their application in finite experience, they are inadequate to express the Ideal, and distort instead of describing its nature. Thus you made use e. g. of the notions of Life, Organism, Self-fulfilling Process. These notions have a determinate meaning in their application to the objects of our limited experience ; but their meaning is itself restricted in that application. The life of any object of our experience is far from being a self-sustaining process, a closed circle of functions revolving free from all external conditions. It is limited in every way, dependent in origin, extent, intensity and duration, and conditioned throughout by what is other and perhaps hostile. No object of our experience *is* Life; and the Life, which some of them manifest, is conditioned by the sources from which it was derived, and by the bodily organs and the environment in and through which it is maintained. Yet the "living whole", which is your Ideal, is to be limited in no way, and in no way dependent upon anything other than itself. Or did you intend to suggest that it came to be, and grew, and would pass away; that it maintained itself in this its bodily vehicle over against an environment not itself? Nor again can the notion of Organism find absolute expression in any of the objects of our experience. No whole is through and through organic, an organism pure and simple. We never find a whole whose parts are what they are as reciprocally ends and means to one another, and such that the plan of coherence (which is the whole) determines absolutely the nature and the being of the parts which in turn constitute it. The idea of such a purely organic whole remains an empty conception, a shadowy notion with no positive significance. To describe your ideal as an "organized experience", if "organized" is used in this absolute sense, in no way elucidates your meaning. And Self-fulfilment, where it applies in our experience, expresses a process which starts with given materials and a given and limited power of working upon them. At best, the process culminates in a limited achievement; and, after a shorter or a longer period of effort and relative success, the Self and its Fulfilment vanish together. Yet you used all these notions to describe your Ideal, with an utter disregard of the

restrictions under which alone they convey a determinate meaning. And the result was meaningless
phrases—words such as "a process, whose moments
sustain the whole, and themselves are made and
constituted by the process", or "a movement, which
is the very substance of the moving elements."'

§ 28. Now it may be admitted that conceptions
derived from partial wholes cannot adequately express
the whole ; and that what we experience is in a sense
always a partial whole, or the whole from a finite and
partial point of view. We cannot experience the
whole completely and adequately, just in so far as
we are not ourselves complete. But because we are
not complete, it does not follow that we are divorced
from the complete and in sheer opposition to it. We
are not absolutely real, but neither are we utterly
unreal. And because our apprehension is restricted,
and in part confused, it does not follow that it is
utterly false and an entire distortion of the nature of
things. The categories which we have to employ
are no doubt inadequate to express the complete
reality ; but this is no reason for not employing them
at all, or for employing them all alike and indifferently.
For they all to some extent express the whole ; and
there are degrees in the relative adequacy of the expression. The categories of Life, Organism, and Self-
fulfilment express in our experience wholes of a more
concrete, more developed and relatively more self-
contained individuality than e. g. the categories under
which we conceive a whole of aggregation, or a whole
constituted by the limiting outline of its continent
environment, or again a whole whose inner being is
a static adjustment of parts or a surface-play of movements between fixed constituent elements. And for
this reason I employed these categories as relatively
more adequate notions under which to conceive the

deal. Still more adequate notions might perhaps have been found within our finite experience. For it would seem that the significant whole, which is truth, can in the end be most adequately described only in terms of the categories of self-conscious thought. But it is worth while to describe it in terms of the categories of Life, Organism, and Self-fulfilling Process as against those lower grades of theory which we have been criticizing—theories which conceive it under the notions of a static whole, like a 'building'; or of an aggregation of units, like a 'sum of truths'; or of a static adjustment of two wholes of fixed elements, like a 'correspondence' between original and copy.

But the real way to meet the charge that the Ideal is inconceivable is to challenge the 'common-sense' attitude of the critic. The Ideal, he is in effect maintaining, is not in its completeness *here* and *now*, and therefore is not actual: it cannot be adequately expressed in terms of finite experience, and therefore is inconceivable. And this criticism betrays an amazing acquiescence in the first hasty assumptions of the unreflecting consciousness. For the critic assumes that finite experience is solid and fully real and clearly conceivable, an unshaken *datum* here and now; and that we must accept it without question as, so to say, a pier from which to throw a bridge across to the cloudland Ideal. But we have been demanding all along an entire reversal of this attitude. In our view it is the Ideal which is solid and substantial and fully actual. The finite experiences are rooted in the Ideal. They share its actuality, and draw from it whatever being and conceivability they possess. It is a perverse attitude to condemn the Ideal because the conditions, under which the finite experiences exhibit their fragmentary actuality, do not as such restrict its being; or

to deny that it is conceivable, because the conceivability of such incomplete expressions is too confused
and turbid to apply to it.

That nothing in our partial experience answers
precisely to the demands of the Ideal, cannot show
that the Ideal is an unsubstantial dream, an idle
play of words. The question is whether our partial
experience through and through involves the being
of the ideally-complete experience which we have
postulated. And the way to answer this question is
to examine the implications of our partial experience,
or on the other hand to trace the Ideal in its manifestations.

§ 29. But this is precisely where our critics will
join issue with us. For they will fasten on the term
'experience', and they will demand, ' *Whose* is this
Ideal Experience? *Where* and *when* is it actual?
What is its precise *relation* to the finite experiences?'

Now one answer to such questions is, ' Such an
experience is nowhere and at no time, no one possesses
it, and it is related to nothing save itself'. For the
questions assume that the Truth is a finished product,
a static consummated whole of experience, which is
somewhere and at some time, exclusive of the finite
experiences as occurrences in time and place, and yet
related to them. But this is not what was meant.
And again they assume that the Truth is the possession
of a finite being. They regard it as the experience of
a 'this-now', much as I may here and now experience
this toothache. But this again was not meant, though
the misleading associations of the term 'experience'
to some extent justify the misunderstanding.[1]

---

[1] The term 'experience' is unsatisfactory, and I should not use
it if I could find a better word. I have endeavoured to guard
against its mischievous associations by coupling it with the
expression 'significant whole'. But if 'experience' tends to

It is not, however, of much value to make a negative answer of this kind. On the other hand, if we answered, 'Such an Ideal Experience is everywhere and at all times; it is the partial possession of all finite beings, and they are the incomplete vehicles of it', we should merely be repeating more explicitly what we have already asserted. The mere assertion is useless; but nothing short of an entire system of metaphysics could serve as its justification. The difficulty, in short, is that our problem is expanding into the whole problem of philosophy, and that the discussion threatens to become unmanageable.

But we must make an effort to discuss the 'relation' of the Ideal Truth to the truth of human judgement and inference without wandering into the field of metaphysical speculation at large. Perhaps the most hopeful procedure will be to start from a few typical instances of 'true' judgement. If we can show their 'truth' expanding in each case into a system of knowledge, and that again as borrowing what truth it possesses from the Ideal Experience which is struggling for self-fulfilment in it, we shall be able to face the difficulties we have raised. We shall be able to face them, for we shall be working with something definite; but we must not assume that we shall be able to solve or remove them.

suggest the experiencing apart from the experience, 'significant whole' tends to suggest the experienced apart from the experiencing. We want a term to express the concrete unity of both, and I cannot find one. For the term 'God', if substituted for 'Ideal Experience', would be seriously misleading in other ways. And superficial criticism, directed against certain travesties of 'Hegelianism', has degraded 'the Absolute' or 'the Idea'—terms in many respects the best for our purpose—until they have become mere conventional symbols for abstractions, which the critic first invents and then dislikes. If we were to employ these terms we should merely excite prejudice, without suggesting the philosophical meaning which they bore in Hegel's system (cf. Hegel, *Encycl.*, III, pp. 464 ff.).

(ii) DEGREES OF TRUTH

§ 30. We are to take a few typical instances of 'true' judgement with a view to showing that their 'truth' *in the end* involves the Ideal which we have described. It will be convenient to select instances typical of two main kinds of judgement, which I shall call respectively *the universal judgement of science* and *the judgement of fact*.[1]

By a 'universal judgement of science' I mean a judgement which claims to express a necessary connexion of content. The judgement '$2+2=4$' asserts that the addition of two units to two units necessarily involves the sum four, i. e. that 'four' is a necessary implication of the content which we express as 'the addition of two and two'. Similarly, the judgement that the external angles of a triangle are together equal to four right angles asserts that, if the external angles of a determinate type of plane figure be conceived as summed, the resultant total is necessarily equivalent to an angle of 360°.

Such judgements would naturally take the form of a hypothetical judgement affirming a necessary nexus between its ground and consequent. But in the instances just quoted there is still retained some matter irrelevant to the nexus affirmed, and the nexus is therefore one-sided only. For though $2+2=4$, yet 4 may result from other conditions than the addition of 2 and 2; and though the external angles of

---

[1] Much of the argument in §§ 30–40 is reproduced (in substance, if not *verbatim*) from my article on 'Absolute and Relative Truth', which was published in *Mind*, N.S., No. 53. I take this opportunity of thanking the editor, Professor G. F. Stout, for permitting me to reproduce an article which owes its origin to a discussion initiated by him ; and of thanking Mr. F. H. Bradley, who made many valuable suggestions when my article was still unprinted.

a triangle are together equal to four right angles, yet it is not precisely *qua* external angles of a *triangle*, but *qua* external angles of a rectilineal figure, that the resultant total angle of 360° is necessarily implied. Hence such one-sided hypotheticals fall short of the typical universal judgement of science. For scientific thinking endeavours to eliminate, from the contents which enter into its judgements, all matter irrelevant to the necessary nexus which they affirm. It does not rest content with the formulation of a hypothetical in which the ground, or the consequent, or both, include elements other than those which precisely condition their interconnexion. It moves towards a formulation in which the two contents are so purified that each necessarily involves the other, neither more nor less.

A 'universal judgement of science', then, is to be conceived as a judgement which naturally takes the form of a *reciprocal* hypothetical. Ground and consequent are precisely commensurate, and the judgement affirms their reciprocal necessary connexion.[1] And we may think of the following as instances: 'Oxygen and hydrogen combined in determinate proportions and under determinate conditions necessarily form water; and water involves precisely such a combination of such chemical elements.' 'If, in a triangle, two of its sides are equal, the two angles opposite those sides are equal; and if, in a triangle, two of its angles are equal, the two sides opposite those angles are equal.' '$3^2 = 9$, and 9 involves 3 as its square-root.' 'The development of such and such a bacillus in an animal organism produces cholera, a disease with such and such symptoms; and wherever there is cholera, a disease with such and such symp-

---

[1] Cf. Aristotle's conception of καθόλου predication, *Post. Anal.* 73 b 25 ff., 74 a 37 ff.; and cf. Bosanquet, *Logic*, Vol. I, pp. 260 ff.

toms, there is such and such a bacillus developing in
an animal organism.'

I have selected judgements of this kind first of all,
because they furnish the strongest support for a view
which would be fatal to the success of our present
endeavour. Every judgement, so it is generally maintained, is either true or false, and what is true is true
always and absolutely and completely. What is true
is *eo ipso* 'absolutely' true. 'Relative truth' is a contradiction in terms, and 'absolute' is an otiose addition to 'truth'. There may be truth about the
Relative; but the truth about the Relative is itself
absolute, i.e. true neither more nor less. A so-called
'partial truth' is a judgement which contains complete
and absolute truth, but which, as compared with another judgement, covers with its truth part only of the
subject-matter of the latter. The same 'partial truth',
looked at from the point of view of the larger judgement, and wrongly taken as equivalent to it, is an
'error'. Hence a 'partial truth' is the same thing
as a true but indeterminate judgement. The determinate judgement is the whole truth about a matter
where the indeterminate judgement affirms only part
of the truth. But the part affirmed is true absolutely
and completely, and remains true to all eternity; it
is the whole truth about part of the matter. It is
added to, increased, supplemented by the determination: but in the supplementation it is not annulled,
nor even altered. Its truth remains, and remains
qua truth precisely what it was. For indeed truth
is timeless, and cannot alter. And in the 'universal
judgements of science', more obviously perhaps than
elsewhere, this view seems evident beyond dispute.
They are abstract, no doubt; but their very abstractness guarantees the precision of their affirmation and
the purity of their truth. The judgement which

affirms the reciprocal implication of the equality of the two sides and of the two angles, expresses only *a part* of the complete knowledge of the isosceles triangle : but, as expressing a part *of knowledge*, it is itself true wholly and without qualification. The reciprocal implication thus affirmed holds unalterably, no matter what fresh implications may be revealed in the contents as knowledge advances. As the science of plane geometry expands into a system, the ' partial truth ' conveyed in such isolated judgements is supplemented and knit together with more and more truths. But though the fuller knowledge holds in its grasp far more of the characteristic properties of the isosceles triangle and far more of its relations to other forms of plane figure, the truth of the original judgement persists as a solid unyielding fragment of the more perfect knowledge. For otherwise, if its truth does not persist, in the progress of geometrical science it presumably becomes false ; and that is a paradox which no one would seriously maintain.

§ 31. At first sight, this view of the matter seems unanswerable, and even obvious. What is once true, it must be agreed, is true always : for truth, since it holds irrespectively of time, holds indifferently at all times. And what is not true is false. Now any science seems full of judgements which are true ; and their truth, like all truth, must be ' timeless ' or ' eternal', and therefore unalterable. The square of three is nine, and nine has three as its square-root ; and this is neither truer, nor less true, *now* than it was in the days of Adam. The conditions of cholera, once precisely formulated, remain for any conceivable expansion of medical science precisely what that formulation affirms them to be. It remains ineffaceably true that the combination of oxygen and hydrogen under the determinate conditions specified in the judgement implies, and is implied by, its commensurate consequent, water. And even if the whole 'situation' does not obtain as full an expression in these judgements as it will obtain with the advancement of knowledge, still a part of it is adequately expressed in them. So far as they go, such universal judgements of science are and remain true, though they may fall short of a full formulation of the conditions of cholera, or of a complete chemical analysis of water.

If we are compelled to accept this contention, the coherence-notion of truth, as we have conceived it, cannot be maintained. For we shall have to recognize that at least the universal judgements of science—whatever may be the case with other judgements—can be possessed of truth complete and final, whether they enter as constituents into any larger whole of knowledge or not. Truth, whatever it might prove to be, would certainly *not* be the self-fulfilling process which is the Ideal Experience. For truth would be found complete and absolute in the isolated judgements, which are mere portions of finite experience. It would be impossible to show that the truth of 'true' judgements is essentially the truth of a system of knowledge; and it would be equally impossible to show that the 'truth' of systems of knowledge 'is borrowed from the Ideal Experience, which is struggling for self-fulfilment in them '.[1] We should be forced to recognize the validity of some such view as that of Descartes. We should be driven to look for the essential nature of truth in the character of the constituent units, and not in the character of the whole of knowledge which they constitute. We should return to the conception of knowledge as a building, in which the bricks and the stones primarily determine the

_____
[1] Above, p. 84.

character of the whole. And the coherence, on which we laid such stress, would be degraded to a mechanical synthesis of secondary importance, a mere external arrangement of the materials, which in no way constitutes their nature.

§ 32. And yet the supposed obviousness of this view fades away before further examination. For what exactly does it maintain? That 'the truth', i. e. the whole complete truth, is timeless and unalterable may be admitted as beyond dispute. But it is an empty admission, if, as we maintain, no judgement in and by itself is adequate to express the complete truth. The judgement $3^2 = 9$ is neither more nor less true now than it was in the days of Adam: but was *it* true then, or will *it* ever be true in that sense of the term? The question is precisely whether the so-called 'truth' of such judgements, *taken with just the meaning they bear in isolation*, is genuine truth, truth timeless and unalterable. Or, rather, the question is whether 'they'—the judgements that we speak of as 'true'—ever were, or are, or could be, isolated in the manner required. And if it be said that the contention is not that any judgement is *the whole truth*, but that any true judgement is *wholly true*, we must doubt whether this distinction will stand examination, or whether those who put it forward quite realize to what they are committed. For how do they conceive the relation of these wholly-true judgements to the whole of truth, these little bits of perfect knowledge to the larger perfect knowledge which they constitute? And how do they conceive the 'truth' either of the single judgements, or of the system of judgements into which they enter?

The theory which we criticized and rejected in our second chapter offers a definite answer to both these questions. For it regards truth and falsity as immediate qualities of ' propositions ' ; and a 'proposition ' is an entity entirely independent of all other entities and of everything mental. A true proposition is possessed in itself of absolute truth as an inalienable quality. And the totality of true propositions is *the truth*, i. e. the absolutely-true whole of all the absolutely-true propositions which are its constituent parts. A 'judgement' is a complex in which a psychical factor is related to a true or false proposition. The relation, indeed, is of a special kind : it is 'the cognitive relation', whose peculiarity is such that one of its terms (viz. the psychical term) '*is* nothing but an awareness of the other term '.[1] Still, the psychical term—the ' belief', or whatever we call it—is a factor independent of the non-mental term which is true or false, although in the 'judgement' the two are related. Hence a ' true judgement' is a misnomer. Strictly, it is the awareness of (or the belief in) a true proposition. The advance of knowledge is presumably the increasing accumulation of beliefs in true propositions. And ideally complete knowledge would be the totality of psychical beliefs in the totality of true propositions, every element in the psychical totality being the awareness of a detérminate element in the other totality.[2]

But we have long ago convinced ourselves that this theory will not hold ; and in any case the advocates of the view, which we are at present examining, are not entitled to borrow their answers from it. For (i) they do not accept the analysis of judgement into a non-mental proposition and a psychical awareness. Truth and falsity are for them predicates of judgement, not qualities of one severed factor in judgement. And this recognition of judgement as the inseparable unity of thinking and the object thought, debars them, as

[1] Cf. above, p. 50,,note.   [2] Cf. above, pp. 35-7.

we shall see presently, from maintaining without inconsistency that any single judgement can in isolation be a fit subject of which to predicate absolute truth. Moreover (ii) they would hardly acquiesce in the conception of knowledge as a totality of beliefs in a totality of true propositions. For such totalities would seem to be aggregates or sums, since each constituent of either totality is absolutely independent.[1] But they profess to regard knowledge as a 'system' of truths; and they mean by a 'system' a whole possessed, in some degree at least, of pervading unity, and not the mere aggregate or *de facto* resultant of the constituent parts.

§ 33. (i) A judgement, as the inseparable unity of thinking and the object thought, is a piece of concrete thinking. The precise nature of its affirmation, its precise meaning, is largely determined by the conditions under which it is made. The judgement occurs in a particular context, it issues from a special background, it concentrates in itself various kinds and degrees of knowledge. Its meaning is coloured by all these determining factors, which together (and with others) constitute the medium of any piece of concrete thinking. The student may use the same words as the master of the science; but the judgement of the latter, though *linguistically* the same as that of the student, conveys a meaning enriched by the whole systematized knowledge which forms the background of his scientific thinking. Such a background is focussed and concentrated, more or less, in every judgement which he makes, or again in every judgement which he 'accepts' from another person. For such acceptance is really an appropriation, which invests the adopted judgement with meaning largely derived from the appropriator's own mental 'back-

[1] Cf. also above, pp. 44–50.

ground'. Every judgement, as a piece of concrete thinking, is informed, conditioned, and to some extent constituted by the *appercipient character*[1] of the mind which makes it, just as what the histologist sees under the microscope is conditioned by the scientific knowledge which has trained his 'eye' and 'informs' his vision; or what the critic sees in a picture, or hears in a symphony, depends upon the appreciative insight which his aesthetic training and his original artistic capacity have contributed to form. To the boy, who is learning the multiplication table, $3^2 = 9$ possesses probably a *minimum* of meaning. It is simply one item of the many which he is obliged to commit to memory. Three times three are nine, just as three times two are six, or as H_2O is water, or as *mensa* is the Latin for table. These are 'truths' which he accepts and must not forget, but which he does not understand. But to the arithmetician $3^2 = 9$ is perhaps a shorthand symbol for the whole science of arithmetic as known at the time. As a piece of *his* concrete thinking, it may signify all that could be read in it and expressed by the best arithmetical knowledge hitherto attained.

And though, in considering the meaning of the universal judgements of science, we are not concerned with the concrete thinking of the individual mind *qua* 'this' or 'that', *qua* differentiated by the idiosyncrasies developed through its particular psychological history; yet we *are* concerned with judgements in which thinking and the object thought are inseparably united. We may refer such judgements to 'the scientific mind' as acts of its concrete thinking,

---

[1] The expression 'appercipient character' was suggested to me by Professor Stout's treatment of 'Apperception' in his *Analytic Psychology*, Book II, chap. viii. But Professor Stout must not be held responsible for the use which I am here making of the idea.

without deciding whether we mean to postulate a universal mind, or merely a purified and typical individual mind. But 'the scientific mind', however vaguely we may use the phrase, at least commits us to the assumption of a determinate and developing 'appercipient character', which charges with a determinate meaning the 'universal judgements of science' wherein it finds its expression. The meaning of any judgement of science is vitally dependent upon the system of knowledge which forms its context, and which is the 'appercipient character' of 'the scientific mind' at that stage of its development. And this appercipient character, as 'the scientific mind' passes through the various stages of its development, undergoes a modification which is far more akin to the organic growth of a living thing than to increase by aggregation or to change by elimination and addition of constituent elements. Or could the change of appercipient character in the scientific mind—as embodied e. g. in the development from the Ptolemaic to the modern system of astronomy—be adequately treated as an affair of *plus* and *minus*, as a dropping out of some judgements and a taking up of others? Or, again, would it be maintained that the discovery of the differential calculus left the contents of 'the scientific mind' unaltered, and merely added fresh elements to the old stock? Has not the entire character of the mathematical mind been changed by the discovery, so that every judgement which it makes is invested with a new significance?

§ 34. I have tried to show that no judgement can comprise its meaning in itself, if 'judgement' signifies a piece of concrete thinking and not an entity independent of mind altogether. The universal judgements of science are abstract, i. e. purified from irrelevancies. The concrete thinking expressed in

them is not the thinking of a 'this-now', not th
thinking of a mind immersed in the tangle of restric
ing conditions, which differentiate it as *my* mind an
my opinions from *your* mind and *your* opinion
Nevertheless it is the thinking of a mind at
determinate level of development; and the scientif
judgements draw their meaning from the system
knowledge which informs that stage of 'the scientif
mind'.

But it may be thought that the arguments whic
I have advanced are too psychological in characte
And though I do not believe that this objection hold
I will try to confirm my position by arguments
a somewhat different kind.

We have seen that the universal judgement
science would most naturally take the form of
reciprocal hypothetical. It affirms a reciprocall
necessary implication of two contents. It states, n
merely that A and B are always found together, b
that, given either, the other *must* be. Now the logic
necessity, which this 'must' expresses, is to bir
together two different contents formulated precise
qua different. For A is not to include any elemen
of B, nor B of A; and yet A in its distinctness is
necessitate B, and *vice versa*. And this is impossibl
except in so far as A and B, whilst definitely distin
from one another, are yet rooted in a common grou
as being the differences of a concrete identity. T
judgement collapses into a tautology unless A and
retain their reciprocally exclusive distinctness; but
loses all rational or logical necessity unless A and
manifest one and the same individual significa
content, as two distinct features in the articulati
of its systematic identity. And indeed the judg
ments, which we quoted as instances, all of th
involve more or less explicitly an identity, with

which their antecedents and consequents are taken, of which these are distinctive features, and on which the necessary connexion between them is based. Two equal angles, if they are equal angles *of a triangle*, necessitate the equality of the two opposite sides, themselves a distinctive feature of that triangle. The multiplication of 3 by itself (within the constitutive conditions of the numerical system, but not otherwise) necessitates 9 ; and if, subject to those same conditions, you take the square-root of 9, the result must be 3. So, the development of the cholera bacillus *must* produce cholera, if both the development and the disease are distinctive modifications of the same determinate identity, viz. an animal organism of a certain type. Or, to put the matter in a more familiar form, every hypothetical judgement involves, and more or less explicitly states, a categorical basis : and only on the assumption of that basis is the affirmation of the hypothetical possessed of meaning.[1] And the basis involved by the universal judgements of science is, *in the end*, when you trace their implications to their ground, that sphere of being which the science in question expresses in the whole system of its reasoning.

§ 35. No universal judgement of science, then, expresses in and by itself a determinate meaning. For every such judgement is really the abbreviated statement of a meaning which would require a whole system of knowledge for its adequate expression. It is this larger meaning, embodied more or less fully in such a system, which, so to say, *animates* the single judgements and gives them determinate significance.[2] To take such a judgement in isolation is to take it in abstraction from the conditions under which alone

---

[1] Cf. Bosanquet, *Logic*, Vol. I, pp. 252 ff. ; *Knowledge and Reality*, ch. i and iii.   [2] Cf. above, p. 16.

its meaning can be determinate: and the restoration of those conditions, i. e. the thinking the judgement in the context which it demands, *eo ipso* modifies the vague indeterminate meaning which it possessed in isolation, if indeed in 'isolation it means anything. For, strictly speaking, it is not possible completely to isolate such a judgement. *Some* categorical basis is involved in every hypothetical judgement, and some 'appercipient character' must inform every piece of concrete thinking. This is not so obvious in the simple instances which we quoted. For the assumptions, e. g. of the numerical system and of Euclidean space with its determinate types of plane figure, have become instinctive to us. The assumptions of these categorical bases, and the 'appercipient character' of the mind therein expressed, are so familiar to us that we take them as a matter of course. Any and every mind, we tacitly assume, approaches the study of the world with the same elementary notions of number and of plane figure, with unquestioning acceptance of the general features of the numerical and spatial systems which underlie our sciences of arithmetic and Euclidean geometry. We take for granted this typical 'appercipient character', and the numerical and spatial conditions of things which it carries with it. But, however right we may be in thus postulating a uniform intellectual background for all judging subjects, we ought not to ignore the control which it exercises on the single judgements. *Because* the categorical basis of the judgement $3^2 = 9$ is identical for all judging subjects, and *because* they all do, as a matter of fact, judge under the assumption of the same basis, we are not *therefore* entitled to isolate the single judgement. $3^2 = 9$, as a scientific judgement, is a piece of the concrete thinking of 'the scientific mind'; and the 'appercipient character' of that mind, even if it be the actual character of all contemporary minds, cannot be left out of the reckoning. The numerical system in its fundamental features is tacitly accepted as part of the framework of the world. It is assumed in every judgement that any one makes about numbers, and in many judgements about other things. But it *is* the categorical basis which the single hypothetical judgements of arithmetic imply, and their meaning is essentially dependent upon it. And the same holds good, *mutatis mutandis*, of the single judgements of plane geometry and *their* categorical basis, viz. Euclidean space.

If we had taken less elementary and less familiar instances the matter would have been more obvious. For the labour required to formulate a universal judgement of science in a more special subject-matter, or the effort of moving through a long process of analysis and demonstration to the discovery of such a judgement in a territory hitherto unexplored, would convince the most sceptical. In such cases, the mind has to be raised to the requisite appercipient level—it has to acquire a certain appercipient character by mastering a system of judgements—before it can formulate the universal judgement in question. And the judgement, when formulated, is devoid of meaning to every one who does not approach it through the system of knowledge in which it has its determinate position. We *suppose* ourselves to understand the judgement $3^2 = 9$, even though we have no intelligent grasp of the system of arithmetical science which it involves: for the terms are familiar, and we possess at least some rudimentary acquaintance with the nature of number. But we could not even *suppose* ourselves to understand an isolated universal judgement of science e. g. in Thermodynamics, or in Trigonometry, or in Physiology, unless we had reached the formulation of the

judgement through the methodical scientific investigation on the results of which it depends. For even
apart from the technicality of the terms in which it
would probably be expressed, the judgement would
bear no meaning for a mind whose 'appercipient character' had not been formed by special study of the
subject-matter in question.

But if no universal judgement of science can be
isolated from its scientific context without losing its
determinate meaning, neither can it, in that isolation,
be 'absolutely true'. For a judgement which is
'absolutely true' must presumably persist as such
even in the ideally complete system which would
express the whole truth.   Doubtless the body of
knowledge, which we call a 'science', falls short of
ideal completeness. But, in comparison with a single
judgement, it is relatively complete and therefore
more nearly adequate to express the whole truth.
Yet in such a body of knowledge the judgement, as
isolated and as possessed of indeterminate meaning,
no longer finds a place. The same form of words
may, or may not, be retained; but the meaning
affirmed (i. e. the judgement) is in the 'science' determinate, and its determination is not a mere external
addition of new bits of meaning to the indeterminate meaning of the isolated judgement. The truth,
which the isolated judgement conveyed to some
extent, but neither wholly nor purely, is more
nearly expressed by it in its context: but 'it in its
context' is not a single judgement, but a system of
judgements.

§ 36. (ii) And this brings us to the second question,
to which we demanded an answer.[1] For the advocates
of the absolute truth of the isolated judgements regard
a 'science' as a systematic whole; and they would

[1] Above, § 32.

repudiate the idea that a sum or aggregate of truths could constitute such a whole of knowledge. Yet, if e. g. in the science of arithmetic there are contained single judgements, each of which is true *per se* without reference to any others, and true *in precisely the same sense* whether taken *per se* or taken as the basis of further judgements which are inferred from it, what becomes of 'the science of arithmetic'? Arithmetic would seem to be a whole, some at least of the parts of which retain in the whole the identical character which they possess *per se*. If so, is the development of a science merely the *addition* of truth to truth? Is geometry neither more nor less than the *aggregate* of geometrical truths; and are the single arithmetical truths merely *collected* into the science of arithmetic, itself the *sum* (or the *class*) of arithmetical judgements? To treat a science as a *sum, aggregate, collection,* or *class* of single truths, each of which is what it is in its single-ness and remains unchanged in the collection, is (I should agree) utterly inadequate as a theory of know-ledge. It is as if one were to treat the Choral Symphony as a *collection* of beautiful sounds, Othello as an *aggregate* of fine ideas, or a picture by Rembrandt as a *sum* of colours and lines. But is not this the logical conse-quence of the view which we are criticizing? No doubt our opponents will deny that they are com-mitted to this unwelcome position. 'Geometry,' they will say, 'is certainly not, on our view, a mere *aggregate* of truths. It is through and through a *system* of truth, and precisely for that reason the parts of that system, the single judgements, must themselves be true. The nature of space reveals itself in every fragment of the Extended. To know a triangle, even if you only know that it is a plane three-sided figure in which equality of two of the sides reciprocally implies equality of the two opposite angles, is *so far* to know the nature of Space. And that knowledge is not altered. As you learn more about the triangle and about other forms of figure, you are indeed increasing and completing your knowledge of Space : but this is to confirm and fulfil your previous knowledge, not to condemn nor in any sense to change it. It is your view (and not ours) which renders it impossible to conceive knowledge as a system. For a system implies elements with determinate natures in determinate relations. But in your system of knowledge which is the relatively complete truth, there are no determinate elements or relations, but all is shifting. Or, if you take the elements as determinate, on your view every one of them is false : and a system of falsities cannot be the Truth. If every note is out of tune—or again if each note shifts its pitch to meet the shifting pitch of each of the others—there will be no symphony. And so, unless 3×3 are 9 and remain 9 unalterably, your " system " of arithmetical truth will be nonsense.'

Now here there seems to be a confusion. For (a) if, in knowing the reciprocal relations of the two sides and angles of the isosceles, I really knew the nature of Space as expressing itself therein, my knowledge of the isosceles would be 'complete', i. e. as full and perfect as geometrical science can make it. It might be called ' absolute ', if it were not misleading to call knowledge of Space (i. e. knowledge of the Universe in respect *only* to its extendedness) absolute. But such knowledge of the isosceles could not be expressed in a single judgement. It would be complete knowledge of Space in its systematic totality, and nothing short of the whole system of geometrical reasoning would be adequate to express it. On the other hand (b) if I know the isosceles only so far as the isolated judgement carries me, in that fragmentary knowledge my grasp of the nature of Space is correspondingly vague and subject to modification. Knowledge of the Whole and knowledge of the Parts, where the Parts form an intimate Whole like that of the spatial system, involve one another. But each involves the other at the same level. Immature knowledge of some or all of the Parts is immature knowledge of the Whole, and full knowledge of the Whole is full knowledge of each and all of the Parts. Nor is the passage from immature to full knowledge the addition of perfect knowledge, bit to bit. The passage is not an increase by aggregation, but a growth by expansion from within.

Certainly a system must be a whole of interrelated elements; and the elements and their relations must have distinguishable and determinate characters. But those characters attach to them, and are determinate, *in the system*: and in the system the elements are certainly not the same as they are outside, if outside they *are* at all. The notes of the symphony must have and retain a determinate pitch: but their pitch is determined by the functions which they fulfil *in the symphony*. In a sense, no doubt, the pitch of the several notes could be fixed in terms of vibrations without reference to the harmonies which they constitute in the symphony. And the single judgements, isolated from their scientific context, or taken in a relatively-immature scientific context, possess *some* meaning and *some* truth. But the nature of the notes, as constituents of the symphony, is through and through determined by their harmonic relations in the symphony, and is in those relations not what it would be if the several notes were sounded in isolation. And the meaning of the single judgements, when they are abstracted from their scientific context, is a caricature —or at best a faint shadow—of their determinate meaning in the system of the science. In that system

alone, where they possess their fullest significance,
do they possess their highest degree of truth.   Hence,
though 3×3 are 9 and remain 9 unalterably, the
significance of this judgement—*and therefore its truth*—
depends upon the numerical system in its totality,
and ultimately upon the character of the Universe
within which the numerical system is a necessary
subject of human thought.

§ 37. The result of the preceding arguments is,
briefly, the following.   Every universal judgement of
science (whatever may be the case with other types of
judgement) is essentially a constituent of a system
of judgements.   The system as a whole affirms a
relatively self-contained meaning, embodies a concrete
and determinate significance.   Any constituent judgement of the system *in vital coherence with the other
constituents* affirms a determinate meaning, because it
is the emphatic and concentrated affirmation of a
distinct, though inseparable, feature of the fuller
significance.   Determinate significance or meaning,
therefore, is the character of the context, within which
every single 'universal judgement of science' has its
logical being and function.   This context, as a concrete
unity of significance, invests the several enunciations—
so long as they are not severed from it—with determinate
meaning: and in the logical continuity or unity of
that context, they are 'pieces of concrete thinking',
i. e. 'affirmations of meaning' or 'judgements' proper,
and not mere sentences or sets of words.   The fuller
significance, which is affirmed in the system of
judgements as a whole, is affirmed in its many
different 'moments' or 'emphases' as the determinate
relatively-partial meanings of the several judgements.
As a *concrete* unity of significance its identity is, so
to say, 'many-faceted', and it can obtain adequate
expression only through the different affirmations

emphasized in the various constituent judgements of the system. Truth is predicable in various degrees of the significance as expressed in the system of judgements, or in the subordinate groups within the system, or in any of the single judgements; and the degree of truth is measured by the degree of fullness of expression which the significance obtains in each case. But though the significance pulsates through all the several judgements of the system, it refuses to be dissected into detached bits of meaning, or to be confined within a single judgement taken in isolation. And *in this sense* no single judgement possesses meaning or truth.

§ 38. The second main kind of judgement, which I propose to consider, may be called the *judgement of fact*. Under this heading I include (*a*) historical judgements, (*b*) descriptive and classificatory judgements, and (*c*) judgements of perception. We may select as typical instances: (*a*) 'Caesar crossed the Rubicon in the year 49 B.C.'; (*b*) 'The native tribes of central Australia regulate their intermarriages by an elaborate totemic system', and 'The whale is a mammal'; and (*c*) 'This tree is green'.

With respect to all these judgements we have to show that their 'truth', so far as they *are* 'true', attaches to them not in isolation but *qua* involving a whole system of judgements. And with respect to all of them, we have once more to meet the contention that they affirm, taken in and by themselves, absolute, final and unalterable truth. For such 'judgements of fact' seem at first sight to stand out against our view even more obstinately than the 'universal judgements of science'. They are absolutely true, it will be urged, under the relations and subject to the conditions (temporal, spatial, and so forth), within which their meaning is affirmed. They state certain facts or events, or certain actual features and relationships of existing things : and their statement is wholly true of *just those* facts and events, or features and relations of actual things. And, further, it is manifest that their truth is unalterable, provided there is no mistake as to *what they affirm*, i. e. as to what 'their truth' is. No doubt the content of such judgements, as they are formulated, is indeterminate. For it is fixed and defined by a complex of relations, which the judgements imply, but which they do not (perhaps could not) fully express within their formulation. Hence the truth expressed in them is vàgue and slight, and capable of infinite further determination. But any further determination—even e. g. that which Omniscience would give to them—*would not alter*, although it would supplement, the truth which they contain for you and me when, and as, we make them.

Caesar *did* cross the Rubicon in 49 B. C. : and this brute fact, enshrined in the series of past events and thus for ever placed beyond the reach of change [1], is affirmed in the judgement. This at least—the *minimum* of meaning affirmed in the judgement—is a grain of solid truth, which nothing can destroy or modify. So too, the native tribes of central Australia *do* regulate their intermarriages by an elaborate totemic system, and the whale *is* a mammal. For, however our interpretation of the native customs may expand and alter, the former judgement expresses an established fact, which our improved anthropological theory must admit and reckon with : and no change in our classificatory system of the animal kingdom can deprive the whale of those characteristics, to the presence of which the latter judgement bears witness. Even if

---

[1] On the principle expressed by Agathon,

'μόνου γὰρ αὐτοῦ καὶ θεὸς στερίσκεται,
ἀγένητα ποιεῖν ἄσσ' ἂν ᾖ πεπραγμένα.'

the whale should become extinct, and the central Australian vanish from the face of the globe, the judgements remain wholly true under the conditions involved in their content. For they never affirmed the perennial existence of their subjects; but only that those subjects, when and as and if they existed, possessed certain attributes.   And the same holds of the judgement of perception.   For if we say 'this tree is green', *this* is doubtless indeterminable for our knowledge, i. e. for our discursive thinking.   Yet, even if Omniscience were to determine *this*, what is true for us of *this tree* (as fixed for us now by perception) would remain true of *this tree* as exhaustively determined by the infinity of relations forming the content of that Omniscience: though no doubt *more* would be true for that absolute knowledge of *this tree* than merely what is now true for us.   Further, *this tree* persists through a period of time and changes its properties.   In the autumn it is brown, in the night it is black, and always (while it exists) it is much besides 'green'.   But still this tree *is* green : and the fact that it is much more besides, and that its greenness changes and vanishes, does not annul nor alter the fact that it is green here and now, viz. under the conditions in which the judgement claims truth.   Nor, lastly, is the truth of the judgement rendered 'relative' by the fact that 'green' is relative to the normal human vision.   For that too is implied in the content of the judgement as affirmed and as claiming truth ; and, if true at all, the judgement is absolutely and wholly true.   We mean to predicate of 'this tree' a quality, which to the present normal human vision appears as 'green' ; and this fact—the fact affirmed in our judgement—will hold, and hold unaltered, even though the appearance would be different to the colour-blind, or to the eye of a fly, or to the normal human vision as it may be two thousand years hence.

§ 39. Yet the judgement of fact, in spite of its apparent solidity and self-dependence, comes in principle under what has been said of the universal judgement of science. What it affirms is subject to a complex mass of conditions unexpressed and yet implied. It draws its meaning and its truth from an inarticulate background of this kind. The judgement of fact, indeed, if it is to affirm *definite* meaning, demands the articulate expression of this background in the form of an explicit system of judgements. And yet in that system the original judgement, as formulated in isolation and as the mere statement of fact, would no longer persist.

The ' brute fact' that Caesar crossed the Rubicon in 49 B. C. is pregnant with significance, owing to the concrete political situation within which it took place. But the actual event was not a nucleus of ' brute fact' encased, solid and distinct, within a surrounding complex of conditions. It was Caesar, at the head of his army and animated by conflicting motives of patriotism and ambition, who crossed. And he crossed the Rubicon at this determinate political juncture, with a full consciousness of the effect of his action on the political crisis at Rome. This—and more—is the meaning of the historical judgement in its proper context, its *definite* meaning. This concrete happening is ' the fact' affirmed in the judgement, if indeed you can arrest the expansion of its meaning even here. We can be sure, at any rate, that the actual happening contains no *bare crossing of a stream by a man in the abstract* as a solid grain of fact, separable from a complicated setting which particularizes it. If the judgement of fact disentangles *this*, and affirms *this* as ' fact' within a context otherwise contributed by inferential construction or historical imagination, it is confusing a mere abstraction with a constituent element of the actual event.

'Well,' I shall be told, 'the brute fact still remains. Caesar *did* cross the Rubicon. You cannot get over that.' But I am not maintaining that the judgement of fact, even when taken at its lowest, is wholly false. It is not wholly false, even when it is as nearly 'isolated' as may be, i. e. when its implied and appropriate context is as little developed as possible. I am only denying that, as thus taken, it is wholly or absolutely true. In the context of a biography of Caesar, the judgement would express a fact revealing Caesar's character: in the context of a history of the decline of the Roman Republic, it would express the death-knell of republican institutions. In either context, the judgement would have a determinate meaning: but in that determinate meaning the 'brute fact'—the supposed meaning of the 'isolated' judgement—would not linger on side by side with additional elements of fact. Such truth as the 'isolated' judgement involves—and every judgement involves *some* truth—'persists' in the fuller truth of the biography or the history, *not* as a pebble persists in a heap of pebbles, but as the first rough hypothesis survives in the established scientific theory.

The descriptive and classificatory judgements fall under the same general principle readily enough. They are possessed of 'truth' in so far as they affirm a determinate meaning, i. e. as 'moments' or 'emphases' of the significance affirmed in a systematic whole of knowledge. Indeed, if we were challenged, we should find it difficult to vindicate their supposed distinction, as 'judgements of fact', from the 'universal judgements of science.' Even the descriptive judgement, as we saw[1], does not *really* profess to be a categorical statement of the actual features of existing things. It *looked* as if it were merely calling attention to the fact that an actually existing tribe actually observes certain interesting restrictions in the intermarriages of its members. But it has not the courage to stake its truth on the actual existence of its subject, and thus it becomes a hypothetical judgement affirming a connexion of content. And of course the classificatory judgement passes at once into the universal judgement of science. ' The whale is a mammal' is no assertion of a *de facto* coincidence of predicate and subject. It means, ' if whale, then mammal,' and challenges that complete purification which would convert it into the affirmation of a *reciprocal* necessary implication.

Nor, lastly, can the judgement of perception stand out against this conclusion. Its definite meaning, or its 'truth', depends upon a 'background' implied in its formulation, and demands articulate expression as a system of judgements. In this respect it falls into line with the other judgements of fact, exhibiting special affinity with the historical judgement. But it differs from the latter in the greater vagueness of its formulation. The context which it demands is most remotely suggested by what it actually says; and the articulate expression of its implied 'background' requires a level of thought far in advance of the level at which the perceptive judgement as such is formulated. Hence the judgement of perception, as such and as formulated, is entitled less than most judgements to claim absolute truth. For it is the product of a comparatively low grade of experience. It does not persist as such and unaltered in the

[1] Above, p. 106.

thought which has risen above the level of everyday conversation, of description of particular matter of fact, and of the practical affairs of life. Even here, indeed, there is more than the judgement of 'this' 'now' and 'mine': and the *more* does not leave the judgement of perception pure and unadulterated and without internal modification. And at any rate it is a totally inadequate vehicle for the expression of knowledge which has any claim to be exact. In the main, and broadly speaking, scientific thought moves in universals. 'This' and 'that', and the distinctions fixed by reference to the individual subject, give place in science to reflective determinations, which are revealed by analysis in the sensuous *datum*, but which are not identical with it. Knowledge, in short, begins with the discovery and the formulation of universal and necessary connexions of content. And the advance of knowledge leaves no vague sensuous subject (no 'this tree'), no vague sensuous attribute, and no mere coincidence of attribute and subject. The more adequate knowledge of 'this tree' is not an accumulation of judgements of perception, but a revolution in which 'this tree' is swept away and determinate connexions between determinate universal concepts are substituted. In the science of botany a judgement of perception like 'this tree is green' finds, *as such*, no place.

§ 40. Nor will it do to protest, 'But the fact expressed in the judgement of perception remains unalterable. For suppose our knowledge to expand until it covers all time and space; suppose even that it becomes Omniscience. Yet, within that complete and all-embracing experience, the original judgement will persist as a clear, if somewhat attenuated, truth— a thread of pure gold within the infinite consciousness.' There is indeed a sense in which this contention is true: but in that sense it hardly seems relevant. Omniscience, we may admit, must be knowledge of everything; and in the infinite experience nothing can be lost. Every fact and every feeling (everything in any sense real), as an element in that experience, is invested with the timeless necessity which defies change or destruction. Nothing, we may agree, is 'lost'; and in this sense the past and the future 'are' no less and not otherwise than the present, error and sin possess the same necessary being as truth and goodness, and there is no difference between the trivial and the important.

But *in what precise sense* is the fact expressed in a judgement of perception unalterable? 'This tree is green' expresses what is matter of immediate experience to you here and now, and to other sentient subjects under the same conditions. It is true within a narrowly restricted area; and beyond that area its truth is liable to modification and perhaps to destruction. The experience, and the expression of it, are no doubt necessary incidents in the world-process, or necessary elements in the infinite experience. But they are 'necessary' precisely as and when and how they occur in the process or subsist in the experience. In so far as the infinite experience is complete and all at once, all the elements thereof are *for the infinite subject* timelessly actual. But in so far as the infinite experience appears as a world-process and unrolls itself in time and space, the elements have that actuality which belongs to them as such appearances, i.e. they occur under determinate limitations of time and place, and not otherwise. Thus the immediate experience and its expression in the judgement of perception are 'unalterable facts' in their actuality, viz. as possessing their determinate position in the series of events. And if the world-process were, so to say, to go back upon itself, and to unroll its series of events afresh from the beginning, these experiences and their expressions would recur in their positions with 'unaltered' actuality. The mummies would walk the earth again, and give expression to their feelings in 'the same' judgements of perception that were passed by the ancient Egyptians: and thus (but not otherwise) the 'unalterable truth' of a judgement of perception might be vindicated. For the judgement 'this tree is green' expresses what is actually matter of direct experience to you and to other sentient subjects. A hundred years hence you and your vision, they and their experiences, 'this' tree and its state, have vanished into the past, and cannot for human knowledge be restored *as such*.

It is irrelevant to insist upon the ineffaceable reality of all the elements of the infinite experience; and it is a confusion to identify their 'reality' as elements in that experience with their 'truth' as entering into the texture of human knowledge. The sentient subjects of the past, their immediate experiences, and the 'truth' of their judgements of perception as expressing those experiences, have as such vanished for us. They are at best for us the precarious products of a most elaborate inferential reconstruction, which in any case can never actually *reinstate* them. The matter of their experiences, in so far as it constitutes the significant content of their judgements, has passed over into the fabric of our knowledge. In that fabric their judgements of perception persist and cling to life. But the distinctive features of those judgements, their individualities, are lost, and the life, to which by a metaphor you may say 'they cling', is not *their* life which they formerly enjoyed. The sciences of botany, of the physiology of the senses, of the physical conditions of colour, &c.—these may be said to absorb and to preserve the 'truth' of such judgements as 'this tree is green'. But the sciences neither contain any judgements of perception *as such*, nor preserve their 'truth' in an unaltered form.

§ 41. In the above hasty survey of certain typical instances of 'true' judgement, I have tried to show *negatively* that no judgement in and by itself is absolutely true; and *positively* that so far as a judgement is 'true' at all, 'its' truth is really the character of a meaning which requires for its adequate expression a system of judgements. No judgement is ever entirely severed from a larger background of meaning, though the background may be relatively obscure except at that portion of itself which is thrown into relief and formulated as *this* judgement. But *this* judgement is 'true' only so far as it is the affirmation of a determinate meaning, i.e. only so far as the relatively-whole meaning of the background, which it implies, emerges as the explicit context fixing the definite bearings of the judgement. The judgement affirms 'its' most determinate meaning (and is, therefore, most 'true') when the background is fully articulate as a system of judgements, into which the judgement in question fits as a determining and determined member. The degree of 'its' truth depends upon the degree of wholeness or self-containedness of the meaning expressed in such a system, i.e. depends upon the completeness of the coherence of the system. And this result seems to confirm the ideal of truth, as we described it in terms of the coherence-notion. For the ideal of absolute truth, by reference to which we are measuring the relative degrees of truth in the various systems of judgements, and (through them) in the single judgements, is the completely individual, self-sustained, significant whole. The truth, we seem to see, emerges in its perfect completeness as an individual meaning with an internal logical connectedness and articulation. Its articulate connexion demands discursive expression as a system of judgements. Its individuality requires self-containedness or complete self-coherence of the system. And this seems to be the ideal, which human knowledge involves and partly attains; though it can never be adequately, fully, or finally embodied within the actual knowledge of finite subjects. For actual human knowledge is never completely self-coherent, if only for the reason that it is growing in time. And if the ideal is never fully embodied in the whole of actual human knowledge, *a fortiori* it refuses to dwell entire within 'a science', and of course *minime* within a single judgement.

§ 42. But in reality we are still far from having established the coherence-notion of truth. The apparent ease with which we have brought together the 'truth' of human knowledge and the ideal of the coherence-notion, is due to a degradation of the latter, and an ambiguity in our account of the former. For we have lapsed into a static conception of the ideal. We have talked complacently as if it were a finished complete whole of truth; and we have made no attempt to dwell on what formerly we emphasized, viz. its dynamic character, as a self-fulfilling life or movement. And if we were challenged as to how *such* an ideal— a rigid, static, finished system—is related to, or implied by, the developing human knowledge, we should find ourselves in an indefensible position. On the other hand we have brought human knowledge nearer to the ideal by a loose and ambiguous use of the terms 'meaning' and 'significance.' A judgement, we said, is 'a piece of concrete thinking,' the 'inseparable unity of thinking and the object thought': and, in virtue of this unity, we regarded the judgement

as affirming 'meaning' or as possessed of 'significance.'[1] But this is not the sense in which the ideal
of the coherence-notion was a 'significant' whole or
a self-contained 'meaning'.

We had agreed that a judgement was no complex
of two independent factors related by the cognitive
relation; and *in this sense*, and by contrast with the
rejected view, we were entitled to speak of judgement
as 'a piece of concrete thinking,' or as 'the affirmation
of meaning'. Further, we had explained that the
meaning affirmed in the universal judgements of
science was freed from the purely personal pecu-
liarities of the psychical medium of *this* or *that* mind's
thinking; and the same freedom might be vindicated
for all the judgements which we considered. Hence
the 'concrete thinking' was not the actual thinking
of *my* mind taken in all the accidental and confused
psychical setting which differentiates it from the
thinking of *your* mind. We were therefore entitled
to assert that a judgement is the affirmation of *universal*
meaning, a piece of the concrete thinking of 'the
scientific mind'. But the 'universal mind' thus postulated—or the typically sane or scientific mind[2]—is
still *subjective* in a sense which I must now try to
make clear.

I do not mean that 'the scientific mind' need be
conceived as the abstract common subject from which
the differences of *this* and *that* mind have been dropped
out, nor as the fictitious individual mind uniting in
itself—by the licence of our imaginative construction—
all the scattered intellectual qualities of the scientific
thinkers whom we admire. It is quite possible to
conceive 'the scientific mind' as a concrete universal
subject, which in 'the pieces of its thinking'—i.e. in
the judgements of science—affirms a meaning universal

[1] Cf. above, pp. 92–9.   [2] Cf. above, pp. 93, 94.

and yet concrete. Such a meaning would demand for its expression the relevant differences of 'emphasis' which attach to the scientific thinking of the different individual men of science. It is a truism that every thinker, in accepting a theory, makes it his own. And the converse ought to be recognized as no less a truism—that every theory, for complete expression of its meaning, must pass through different minds and manifest in itself the many 'emphases' of their intellectual individualities.

But still 'the scientific mind' is *over against* a reality to be known, and its 'concrete thinking' is *about* something other than the thought. We may speak of a judgement of science as an 'inseparable unity of thinking and the object thought': but we must interpret *object thought* as the content of the thinking, or as the *what* of which the actuality of the thinking is the *that*. The 'meaning', in short, is still adjectival. It is a predicate, which, in the judgement or system of judgements, is 'affirmed of', or 'referred to', reality. It is, to use a somewhat crude metaphor, neither on earth nor in heaven, but suspended midway between. Not on earth; for it is freed from the irrelevant psychical setting, which would constitute it an actual thought occurring as a term in the series of modifications of an individual's consciousness. And it is not in heaven; for it is not substantial, but a 'wandering adjective' waiting to be joined to the substantial reality.[1]

§ 43. The system of judgements which we have shown to be involved in the single 'true' judgements is a body of knowledge *about* reality. It is a 'meaning' in the sense of a logical content, not in the sense in which the ideal of the coherence-notion (the 'significant whole') is 'meaning'. We started, in fact, from the

[1] Cf. F. H. Bradley, *The Principles of Logic*, Bk. I, chap. i, §§ 2–12.

position of current Logic. We assumed the finite
knowing subjects, and over against them the reality
to be known. We recognized a 'universal' or 'typical'
scientific mind as the subject, whose concrete thinking
is judgement as affirmation of meaning. But the
meaning thus affirmed is a mere 'logical idea,' a
'floating adjective,' a shadowy tissue of knowledge
between the knowing subjects and the reality. Even
if we could maintain that, as the concrete thinking
of 'the scientific mind', it has secured a lodgement
in an actuality, still it remains subjective; for it is
a qualification referred to the reality, and not the
substantial reality itself in its self-fulfilment. An
articulate whole of 'meaning' in this sense of the
term cannot be 'true' in the manner demanded by
the coherence-notion. For it refers beyond itself, and
cannot, by the very conception of it, be self-sustaining
or self-complete. Its 'coherence' would be a mere
formal consistency, which would leave the solid reality
out. It inevitably suggests *correspondence* in some form
as the standard of its 'truth'. And we have failed to
show that the 'truth' of human knowledge is a
'symptom' of the ideal truth, which we described in
terms of coherence. We have failed to show that the
substantial significant whole expresses itself both in
our knowledge and in the reality known, as the
ground of that 'correspondence' which we employ
in our finite experience as a sign of truth.[1]

But though we have failed, we can perhaps see
more clearly the reason of our failure, and thus
prepare for a fresh attempt. We started from the
finite experiences, and tried to show that their 'truth'
was in the end derived from the ideal experience.
We hoped by this method to show *both* that the
ideally-complete truth, as conceived by the coherence-

[1] Cf. above, pp. 16, 17.

notion, was no idle speculative dream, but the solid
substantial life of the actual finite experiences ; *and also*
that the measure of their actuality and 'truth' was to
be found in the ideal. And we failed, because, in
starting from the finite experiences, we took them for
granted in their apparent independence of the ideal.
We assumed the severance between the finite thinkers
and the real world, which they think about and
endeavour to know. And even when, by an effort,
we got free from the psychical machinery of their
thinking [1], we were still moving in a sphere, where

[1] I do not inquire *how* the logician can pass from the
'psychological individual' to the 'logical subject', from *this*
actual thinking (with all its psychical machinery and particular
setting) to the thought which claims truth as affirming universal
meaning. The logician, I am convinced, never really starts with
this individual thinker in the sense supposed ; and, if he did, the
passage from this psychological fiction to the subject of knowledge
would be impossible and beyond all explanation. The distinction
(which e. g. F. H. Bradley has used) between 'idea' as *psychical
image* or *symbol* and 'idea' as *logical content*, is valuable as a statement of the sense in which the logician speaks of ' idea '; and
presumably it was never intended for any other purpose. The
solipsistic individual, conscious originally of a succession of
psychical events as his own, and conscious of these alone, is
a discredited relic of subjective idealism, and no logician can
be asked to explain by what process these psychical events are
converted into logical contents or universal meanings. If the
psychologist chooses to postulate such a stream of psychical
events as the machinery of the individual's thinking, that is
his affair, though we may think his psychology strangely antiquated. But if the psychologist calls these events 'images' or
'symbols', we must be on our guard. For this 'psychical
imagery' is not *what* the subject thinks, but the supposed
machinery of his thinking ; just as the inverted image on the
retina is not *what* the subject sees, but part of the supposed
physiological machinery of his vision. The 'images' or 'events',
in short, in so far as they are the machinery of thinking, are
neither images nor events *for the thinker.* And when the subject
thinks of the psychological machinery of his own thinking, the
'images' or 'events' which he studies are universal, like all
objects of thought, and no longer the perishing terms in the
unique series which is supposed to constitute *his* stream of consciousness. The psychical events or images, in fact, are *now*
events and images *for* him, and *for* any other mind if he chooses

the separation between the knowing mind and the reality known is fundamental and not to be overcome. Within such a sphere, 'truth' inevitably implies two factors; and so long as the duality is maintained, some form of the correspondence-notion is the only possible theory of truth. It appears to be the general opinion that knowledge essentially involves a duality of this kind, and that the logician must work within a sphere thus irremediably divided. Hence current Logic, consciously or unconsciously, employs the notion of truth as correspondence, and, if that notion be challenged, throws the burden of justification on Metaphysics.

§ 44. But Metaphysics cannot acquiesce in the severance of finite thinkers from one another, nor in the severance of the judging mind from that about which it judges. And if the maintenance of such a duality is necessary for current Logic, then *either* current Logic must be superseded by a new Logic working within a hypothesis which Metaphysics can accept; *or* it must be recognized that Logic, as a partial science based on a fictitious assumption, formulates conclusions which are not merely *pro-*

to describe them; and his thinking of them requires (on the supposed psychological theory) another stream of events as its machinery. And if it be admitted that 'image' is a misleading expression, and 'symbol' be preferred, I should still distrust the theory. For is the stream of psychical events symbolic of the logical contents *by convention*, as a system of marks traced on paper symbolizes a system of significant sounds? If so, then the subject must know the set of symbols and the set of symbolized meanings together with the principle of their correspondence, if the 'psychical events' are to symbolize anything for him; and *this* knowledge will be inexplicable on the theory. Or does the psychical symbol suggest the logical idea—the universal meaning —*naturally*, as the rosebud suggests the rose? If so, then the universal meaning is itself present in, and as, the psychical 'symbols'; and we shall have recognized that the 'psychological individual', with his purely particular stream of purely particular 'ideas', is an unwarranted fiction.

visional only, but also of necessity to a large extent false. For the notion of truth, which it employs as its standard, is inadequate and—unless modified in the light of the coherence-notion—wrong. But it cannot be so modified until the duality, on the maintenance of which its whole procedure is based, is discarded. It is not enough to say : ' We, as logicians, work with the correspondence-notion of truth. We admit that this notion is inadequate. But we trust to Metaphysics to establish the ideal of coherence as the basis which supports and justifies the " truth " of correspondence '. This is not enough, unless a continuous passage can be shown from that conception of things, which renders the coherence-notion possible, to the dualistic conception which is involved in ' correspondence '. And it hardly seems possible to do this without fundamentally reconstructing current Logic. For it is essential to the coherence-notion that there should be *no severance*, no unpassable gulf, between the judging mind and that about which it judges ; but it is essential to the correspondence-notion that this severance should be, and be maintained.

Yet it is impossible to leave Metaphysics and current Logic in this irreconcileable antagonism. Logic, no doubt, is primarily the theory of finite thinking : and the truth achieved in such thinking is partial, relative, and imperfect. But it is recognized as thus deficient, and the degrees of its relative perfection or imperfection are measured. And this implies in the finite thinker—and in the Logic which reflects upon finite thinking—the possession of absolute truth in some form. We cannot, then, escape the difficulty by saying that Logic *is* a partial science, concerned with human knowledge only and employing an imperfect ideal of truth. For human knowledge is essentially the knowledge of a mind in some sense possessed of absolute truth ; and Logic itself, in recognizing the imperfection of the corre-spondence-notion, implies the grasp of the perfect notion.

The only solution, it would seem, must lie (a) *on the part of Logic*, in a more frank recognition of the purely provisional character of its dualistic assumptions, and of the *modal* nature of the knowing mind as the subject of knowledge ; and (b) *on the part of Metaphysics*, in an attempt to show the negative element in the ideal experience.   Metaphysics, in other words, must endeavour to reveal the relative independence of subject and object as essential to the very nature of the ideal, thereby furnishing the relative justification of the correspondence-notion of truth.

CHAPTER IV

The Negative Element and Error

§ 45. There is a side of our subject which we have hitherto neglected, and this neglect is perhaps the chief cause of our failure to grasp the nature of truth. Moral goodness lives in the contest with evil; physical health emerges in contrast to disease and often in the triumph over it. And neither the moral philosopher nor the physiologist can afford to neglect these 'negative' elements. Similarly—at least in human experience—truth is everywhere confronted with falsehood, and error is the inseparable shadow of knowledge. The antagonism is vital to the nature of the conflicting contraries, and neither can be understood apart from the other.

We have already seen reason to think that there is a fundamental opposition of some kind in the very heart of things. For ideal experience, as we saw, must be conceived dynamically and not statically; as a living, self-fulfilling process, not as a rigid structure or a finished quiescent whole. And all movement, process, and life most certainly involve a negative element.[1] They exhibit a 'being', which emerges in contest with a 'not-being'. They manifest an identity which perhaps overcomes otherness and difference, but assuredly does not extinguish them.

[1] Cf. above, pp. 76, 77. I am not suggesting that a quiescent systematic whole could *be* apart from a negative element. All system essentially involves distinction and negativity. But this is, *a fortiori*, manifest in ideal experience, if it is a system which must be conceived under dynamical categories. Cf. also below, pp. 137, 138.

The opposition between subject and object, the maintenance of which human knowledge demands, and the genuine (if relative) independence of these two factors, suggested the same conclusion to us from another side. We can no longer acquiesce in the view that, while evil and error exist of necessity ' on earth ' as the antagonists of goodness and truth, 'in heaven' there is pure affirmation.[1] We are committed to the recognition of a negative element in ideal experience itself, and of some form of otherness in the very being of truth which will justify the relative independence of subject and object within human knowledge.[2] The only question for us is as to the exact nature of this negative element, this fundamental opposition in the heart of things ; and we take up the study of Error and kindred matters with the hope of finding an answer.

§ 46. It will be as well to lay down an obvious distinction at the outset. I will state it in the traditional terms, without at present attempting to define them further. The opposition, with which we are concerned, is an opposition of contraries, not of contradictories. Evil—the wrong in conduct—is the contrary of the right. Error—the false in knowledge— is the contrary of the true. Evil falls within the moral sphere as the expression of a deliberate moral will. Its antagonism to the right is the hostility of a positive opponent, not the sheer absence of moral quality ; for that is a bare negation which removes the act in question from the sphere of conduct

---

[1] Cf. Plato, *Theaetetus*, 176 A Ἀλλ᾿ οὔτ᾿ ἀπολέσθαι τὰ κακὰ δυνατόν, ὦ Θεόδωρε—ὑπεναντίον γάρ τι τῷ ἀγαθῷ ἀεὶ εἶναι ἀνάγκη—οὔτ᾿ ἐν θεοῖς αὐτὰ ἱδρῦσθαι, τὴν δὲ θνητὴν φύσιν καὶ τόνδε τὸν τόπον περιπολεῖ ἐξ ἀνάγκης. διὸ καὶ πειρᾶσθαι χρὴ ἐνθένδε ἐκεῖσε φεύγειν ὅτι τάχιστα. Plato himself exhibits a profounder insight elsewhere. Cf. e. g. *Sophist.* 254 B–259 B.

[2] Cf. above, pp. 115 ff.

altogether.[1] Similarly, the false in matters of knowledge, the error with which we are here concerned,
is a determinate opinion in positive antagonism
to the true. The mathematician e. g. may be 'ignorant' in respect to chemistry, in the sense that
for him chemical phenomena simply are not. This
kind of 'ignorance' is the sheer absence of apprehension, the gap in consciousness, to which Plato
assigned τὸ μὴ ὄν as the correlative sphere. It is
not false thinking or error, the contrary opposite of
truth.[2]

§ 47. We can proceed at once to consider a view of
error which is connected with the correspondence-
notion of truth. A judgement, Aristotle tells us[3], is
true if it unites or separates according as things are
really conjoined or dissevered. And a judgement is
false if it unites where really there is severance, or
separates where really there is union. Hence we

---

[1] 'Sins of omission' mean, in ordinary usage, failures to do
certain things to which we recognize a moral obligation. They
are contraries of right, not contradictories. If I recognize a duty
to love my neighbour, it is contrary to right to disregard his
existence, or to 'omit' the courtesies and kindnesses which neighbours expect. The failure to carry out my recognized duty is
in principle morally wrong, even though I stop short of positive
injury. But if there is a mere gap in my moral consciousness,
so that I am simply unaware of any duty towards my neighbour,
this 'omission' itself, as a sheer absence, is *morally* nothing,
however much I may be to blame for conduct which has thus
paralysed my moral vision.

[2] Cf. Plato, *Rep.* 476 E ff. And cf. Aristotle's conception of
the immediate grasp of τὰ ἀσύνθετα, in respect to which ἀπάτη (error)
is impossible. The mind either thinks them, or simply does not
think them. In the first case, we apprehend them, and our
apprehension is *eo ipso* true; for it is a grasp or a contact, in
which mind and its object are one. They—pure forms without
matter—are present wholly, in their undivided singleness, as the
content of our thought. In the second case, there is sheer ἄγνοια,
a contradictory not-grasping. The forms are not apprehended,
i. e. there is a gap in the content of our thought. (Cf. *Metaph.* Θ.
10, *De Anima*, 430 a 26 ; b 26, ff.)

[3] Cf. e. g. *Metaph.* 1027 b 18 ff. ; 1051 a 34 ff.

judge truly if our thought corresponds to the real state of things; and we err if our thinking is in a condition contrary to that of the reality. If the cohesion or the severance of the real things is conditioned solely by their essential nature, and is therefore timelessly actual or necessary, the truth is a 'necessary' or 'eternal' truth. But if the cohesion or the severance is due to extraneous conditions, and is temporary, the same judgement will change from true to false according to the change in its real counterpart.

In reality e.g. Man is a composite whole, the constituent elements of which reciprocally involve one another and thus eternally cohere. The affirmative judgements 'Man as such is rational,' or 'Man is essentially animal', unite predicates with their subject so that the union corresponds to the eternal cohesion of elements in the real whole. Therefore these judgements are necessary and eternal truths; and the negative judgements, dissevering 'animal' or 'rational' from 'Man', are false. The square is a composite whole, the constituent elements of which—its sides, its angles, its diagonals, &c.—cohere eternally in determinate relations; and 'commensurability' is eternally dissevered from the diagonal in relation to the side. Hence the negative judgement, 'the diagonal of a square is not commensurate with the side,' separates a predicate from a subject so that the ideal severance corresponds to an eternal divorce in the real things. Therefore this negative judgement is a necessary eternal truth, and the affirmative judgement uniting 'diagonal' and 'commensurability' is false. Finally, the real Socrates at times is really ill, at times illness is really apart from him. Hence the judgements 'Socrates is ill,' 'Socrates is not ill,' change from true to false or from false to true according as they agree or disagree with the temporary cohesion or severance in actual fact.[1]

§ 48. A theory of knowledge which is content to accept the correspondence-notion of truth as ultimate stands for us already condemned. We need not repeat our criticism; but we may confirm it, by exhibiting the helplessness of such a theory in face of the problem of error. For, let us consider. When we think truly, there is a real complex, a real one-of-many, constituting the exact counterpart of the one-of-many which is our judgement. When we think falsely, how is our judgement related to the 'real things'? Is there *no* counterpart in reality to the false judgement? Or is there a real counterpart? and if so, in what sense?

(i) 'The diagonal of the square is commensurate

---

[1] The reader will kindly bear in mind that my primary object is to examine a certain *type* of theory, not to expound in all their details the views which Aristotle actually put forward. I believe that the above account is substantially accurate; but it is difficult to be confident, owing to the brevity and obscurity of some of the passages in question. I cannot enter here into Aristotle's interesting attempt to show that the cohesion of the essential elements in a composite substance is ultimately to be conceived dynamically, as the formation of a ὕλη, or as the actualization of a δύναμις (cf. *Metaph.* z. 12, and H. 6). Assuming that this attempt is successful, the Substance at this level of its unity would be the counterpart of νόησις (intuitive apprehension), and not of judgement. The complexes, which Aristotle regards as the real counterparts of judgements, are possessed of a lower level of unity. So far as one can judge by his instances, the 'things', whose relations the judgement faithfully presents or distorts, are a Substance and one of its Attributes, viz. either an element in the essential nature of the Substance, or a *proprium* or a συμβεβηκός of the Substance. One would expect the true affirmative judgement to represent a connexion between two elements within the Substance or complex whole, rather than a connexion between the Substance and one of its elements. But in that case there would be nothing in the real counterpart exactly corresponding to the distinction between subject and predicate in the judgement. And this would probably be a serious difficulty to Aristotle, since (as we know from *Post. Anal.*, p. 83 a) the logical relation of subject and predicate represented for him a real relation of inherence of attribute in substance.

with the side' is a false judgement. It is false, let us suppose, because there is no real counterpart of it. There are squares, and sides of squares, and diagonals; and, again, there is commensurability. But there is no square so constituted that the relation of commensurability holds between its diagonal and its side. Hence to the separate constituents or materials of the judgement, there correspond real elements; but to the judgement as a whole, there corresponds nothing real. Error consists in this form of combination of the material elements of thought, which represents nothing. The false judgement, taken in its entirety as this form of combination of these materials—and, unless so taken, it is neither a judgement nor false—is the thinking which has nothing for its object. Error is thinking the thing which is not. False thinking is the thinking of nothing.

Now the theory started with the assumption that thinking was the ideal representation of the real. And though error misrepresented the real, it was still the real which was misrepresented. Yet to 'think of nothing' looks uncomfortably like 'thinking nothing', i. e. not thinking. And if we are put to it, we must certainly agree with Plato that the man who judges falsely, undoubtedly thinks, and thinks something.[1] But perhaps we have made an unfair use of the ambiguous term 'nothing'.[2] For we must distinguish between thinking-nothing in the sense of not-thinking, and thinking-nothing in the sense of thinking of a reality which is negative.

[1] Cf. Plato, *Theaetetus*, 188 D ff.
[2] Cf. Lewis Carroll, *Alice through the Looking-glass*: 'Who did you pass on the road?' the King went on, . . . 'Nobody,' said the Messenger. 'Quite right,' said the King: 'this young lady saw him too. So of course Nobody walks slower than you.' 'I do my best,' the Messenger said in a sullen tone. 'I'm sure nobody walks much faster than I do!' 'He can't do that,' said the King, 'or else he'd have been here first.'

(ii) We are to suppose, then, that in a sense there is a real counterpart of the false judgement. Error is the thinking the thing which is not; but 'the thing which is not' is yet real. It is a negative reality. Now, a true negative judgement, according to the theory, is also a thinking the thing which is not. For if I judge 'the diagonal is *not* commensurate with the side of the square,' my judgement is true; and it is true because my thought of the not-being of commensurability has as its corresponding counterpart the real absence of this relation. The severance, which my negative judgement effects between the ideal elements, corresponds to a real disunion of the elements in the real whole. The 'judicial separation' expresses a real divorce. Hence the true negative and the false affirmative judgements are 'about' the same real counterpart. Their difference consists in their contrary attitude towards the same reality.[1] The false affirmative judgement thinks that to be which really is not, whilst the true negative judgement correctly thinks it not to be. Error is not due to the absence of a real counterpart of the judgement, but to the discordance of the counterpart and the thought.

But we have gained nothing by this attempt to defend the theory. For (a) the conception of a 'negative reality', which we have drawn into relief, is precisely that which has to be explained.[2] And (b) even if this conception can be justified, error is *the discordant thinking of this negative reality.* The thinking what is real in a way in which it is not real, this, and nothing short of this, is error. And we have not shown that there is any real counterpart to this *discordant thinking* in its entirety. Hence error remains a 'thinking-nothing' in the sense which seemed to conflict with the basis of the theory.

[1] Cf. Aristotle, *Post. Anal.* 89 a 23–37.   [2] See below, § 50.

Perhaps this last point may be made clearer if we consider a false negative and a true affirmative judgement. It is true that 'the angles at the base of an isosceles triangle are equal to one another,' because (I presume) in the real counterpart of our judgement the angles are really united by the relation of equality. It is false that they are not equal. For to think thus is to judge discordantly with the real counterpart, since it is to think *that* 'equality' not to be which actually obtains. Now the counterpart of the true judgement is here the being of equality within a complex; and the counterpart *demanded* by the false judgement is the not-being of equality within that complex. But if the demand were satisfied, the false judgement would be true; for it would represent fact. It is false just because the not-being which it demands *is not*, i. e. just because *nothing* corresponds to it.

§ 49. The above discussion may appear somewhat sophistical. 'Your criticism,' we may be told, 'is valid only against an antiquated form of the correspondence-theory of knowledge. Nobody would now accept so crude a formulation of the relation between thought and reality.'

Now a certain air of unreality does undoubtedly pervade all examinations of this type of theory. For the whole attitude which is being criticized belongs to a superseded level of thinking. Hence any exposition or discussion is apt to appear like a caricature. But I believe that the correspondence-notion of truth logically carries with it the conclusion which we have reached, viz. that error is the thinking of nothing. And I will try to show that this is so.

We are to suppose (if I understand the position rightly) that thought and reality are two spheres, each a one-of-many-elements, which confront one another. A judgement is true when its structure is identical with the structure of that portion of reality to which it, as a portion of thought, refers. This identity of structure is 'correspondence', and it means that for every different element in the thought-complex there is one, and only one, determinate different element in the real-complex. On such a view, error must mean either the presence of an element or elements in the judgement, to which nothing answers on the side of reality; or *vice versa* the presence of an element or elements in the real, without any elements in the judgement to match them. Error, that is to say, is a 'too-much' or a 'too-little' in the thought; and either alternative means a sheer nothing, a mere gap, on one side or the other. The error which is a 'too-much' involves elements in the judgement which are thoughts of nothing. The error which is a 'too-little' involves real elements which are nothing to the erring person's thought, since in his judgement there is no thought of them.[1]

But we must be careful here, lest we fall into confusion. We have been speaking of error without sufficiently distinguishing. *A*'s error, as it is for *A* while he is in error, is one thing; but *A*'s error as

---

[1] I have not forgotten the discussions in chapter i (cf. e.g. §§ 6, 8, 9); but I do not see how the recognition that the 'real' must be *for* the judging subject in some sense (e.g. in the form of feeling) affects the present question. For, if the correspondence-theory be thus modified and refined, *all* thought, true and false alike, is confronted with a content in the form of feeling. The 'correspondence', which is truth, holds between two factors within consciousness; and so does the 'discordance', which is error. And the only possible distinction between the two is (so far as I can see) that either on the real-side or on the thought-side —either in the content *qua* felt or in the content *qua* judged— there is, in the case of error, a gap. The view that error is not the thought of nothing, but the thought of one thing instead of another (i.e. that the 'discordance' is displacement or disorder of the elements), will be considered presently.

it is for B, the person who recognizes that A is in error [1], is quite another thing. So long as A is in error, the gaps on either side are simply nothing *for him*; the superfluous elements in the real simply are not at all, and the superfluous elements in his judgement are not 'superfluous', since *for him* there is no failure in the corresponding real, but a sheer unrecognized gap. A's error, therefore, while he is in error, is *for him* neither a 'too-much' nor a 'too-little'. On the other hand, A's error *for B*, if B recognizes it as error, is a 'too-much' or a 'too-little'. B's thought, we may suppose, exactly coincides with the reality for him; or, in B's mind, the content *qua* judged exactly corresponds with the content *qua* felt. In his completer knowledge, A's gaps (on one side or the other) have been supplemented. B sees as *deficiencies*, which in his own mind have been made good, *the absences* which were in A, but which *to A* were nothing at all.

The result of this distinction is somewhat paradoxical. For it seems to follow that if A is to err, his state of mind must be *for him* true. If A's error were error *for him*, he would have passed beyond it on the way to truth. For it was B, as we saw, who recognized A's error *as* error; and the condition of this recognition was that B himself should have overcome and supplemented A's error in his own completer knowledge.

Are we to infer that error is nothing but a superseded stage in the development of truth? That it has no being except within the wider knowledge which corrects it? When I am in error, I am *for myself* judging truly; and though subsequently I may realize that I was in error, my error has then become for me a subdued portion of a fuller truth. As error it exists

---

[1] Or 'A's error as it is for A himself, when his knowledge has advanced and he recognizes that he was in error.'

for me only in the past. And even when the past was present, it was not error *for me*, but only *for you*, within whose fuller knowledge it was a deficiency made good, an error which had lost its sting.

Whatever may be the value of this suggestion, we cannot pursue it further at present.[1] We must return to the correspondence-theory. Error, we have seen, is for that theory a 'discordance' between thought and reality, or between a content *qua* felt and *qua* judged; and the 'discordance' involves a sheer nothing on one side or the other. And this is incompatible with the initial assumption that thought represents or misrepresents the real. For a sheer nothing on the side of the real can neither be represented nor misrepresented; since, *ex hypothesi*, for the thought in question it is nothing at all. And a sheer nothing on the side of the thought neither represents nor misrepresents; for it is not thinking at all.

We might indeed attempt to regard error as a judgement in which, although all the elements had their real counterparts, the inner structure was other than that of the real. The false judgement would be a one-of-many having a real one-of-many as its counterpart, but having its 'many' displaced. The inner detail in the judgement would be arranged in the wrong order. We should think in the form $B\,A\,D\,C$, where the real counterpart was $a\,\beta\,\gamma\,\delta$. Error would be the thinking one thing in place of another, where the thought-elements had real counterparts, but the thought-arrangement was confused, i.e. discordant with the real arrangement.[2]

But the whole notion is too vague to help us. For if my thought contains elements, every one of them

---

[1] See below, §§ 51 ff.

[2] Cf. Plato, *Theaetetus*, 189 b ff. (ἀλλοδοξία), and 197 b ff. (ἡ τῶν ἐπιστημῶν μεταλλαγή).

having a counterpart in the real whole, *any* order in which they are arranged in my thought will result in 'correspondence' between the two wholes, provided the several elements on either side are thereby coupled one-to-one. The arrangement $BADC$ fulfils this condition as well as e.g. $ABCD$ or $ADBC$; i.e. $BADC$ is a 'true', and not a 'false', judgement. Before the theory is entitled to speak of a 'wrong' or 'confused' order, of a 'displacement' or a 'thinking one thing instead of another', it must provide us with a more exact determination of the kind of 'correspondence' constituted by the 'right' order.

If indeed the elements on either side determinately involved one another in a determinate order, the case would be different. The real would be a genuine whole whose elements cohered, by the immanent necessity of their nature, within the unity of plan of the whole; and the judgement $BADC$ would similarly be a genuine, though quite different, whole. But then, in what intelligible sense could the judgement possess counterparts of its elements in the real? The A in the judgement would not have the α in the real as its counterpart; for the 'real' α is essentially a constituent of $\alpha\beta\gamma\delta$, and of this alone. It is essential to the 'real' α that β—a β followed by γ, and a γ followed by δ—should succeed it. And this order of succession, essential to the real whole, and entering deep into the being of its elements as the unity of plan which makes the many 'one', in no way enters into the being of the element called 'A' in the thought-whole. *That* is essentially preceded by B, and followed by a D which precedes C; and, as a constituent of this quite other structural plan, A is essentially bound up with $BADC$ and with this alone.[1]

[1] The above argument of course assumes that a 'genuine'

§ 50. We have left the conception of a 'negative
reality' unexamined and unexplained; and we have
contented ourselves with showing that, with or without it, error constitutes a problem which the correspondence-theory of knowledge is unable to digest.
But it will repay us to investigate this conception now.

It is not difficult to see how Aristotle was led to
postulate a 'negative real' as the counterpart of the
true negative judgement; and, however crudely he
has formulated his view, it rests on a certain basis
of truth. If we regard the judgement as a synthetic
activity of the individual mind combining two 'ideas'
into a single thought in which their union is affirmed
or negated[1], it is evident that the truth or falsity of
the judgement must lie in its reference to a reality
other than the act of judging, i.e. other than the judgement itself. And if, further, this *other* is identified
with a reality independent of thought altogether—the
natural result of the tacit assumption that thought is
nothing but the individual's act of judging[2]—the next

whole—a whole of the kind in question—cannot consist of
'independent' elements combined by 'external' relations. Cf.
above, §§ 15–17.

[1] Cf. Arist. *de Interpr.*, 16 a 9 ff.; *de Anima* 430 a 26 ff.;
Metaph., 1027 b 17 ff. On the whole subject, consult Maier, *Die
Syllogistik des Aristoteles*, Part I, especially pp. 24 ff.

[2] No doubt Aristotle did not acquiesce in the somewhat crude
dualism which his theory of the truth and falsity of the judgement
involves. Thus e. g. his use of the distinction between immediate
or intuitive apprehension (νόησις) and mediate or discursive thinking (διάνοια, λόγος), and his conception of θεωρία as the ἐνέργεια of
which ἐπιστήμη is the δύναμις (cf., perhaps, *Metaph.*, 1087 a 10 ff.;
De Anima, 417 a 21–9), indicate a serious endeavour towards
a more satisfactory view. The reality, which is *other than* judgement, is grasped by νόησις, and thus is not 'independent' of
thought; and the abstractly universal knowledge, attained in
scientific demonstration, culminates in the intuition in which
knowing and known are inseparable sides of the one individual
'truth' or 'reality'. But the bulk of his theory of knowledge
proceeds as if his conception of the truth and falsity of the judgement were final; and I see no evidence that he was prepared to

step follows very simply. For the 'reference' can be nothing but correspondence, representation, repetition of structure, or mirroring; or, if the judgement be false, discordance, misrepresentation, displacement, or distortion. And since, in the synthetic activity which *negates* the union of two ideas, I at times attain to truth, there must be ' negative realities' (i. e. complex wholes involving a real severance between their elements) as the 'other' to which such negative judgements refer. If my true judgements repeat the structure of the real, the real on the other hand is such as to be repeated in the structure of my true judgements. And thus, from the fact of true negative judgements, we must infer the being of 'negative realities' in the sense explained.

Aristotle's formulation of his theory seems strange and crude because he appears to treat the negative and affirmative truths, and their corresponding realities, *on the same level*. He speaks as if 'the diagonal is incommensurate with the side of the square' were a truth as final and significant as e.g. 'the interior angles of a triangle are together equal to two right angles'; and as if the real counterparts of the two judgements were each, equally and alike, a coherent self-dependent entity. But the negative judgement in question is not far above the level of the 'infinite' judgement (the negative of bare exclusion), and is invested with a *minimum* of significance. It is raised above this vanishing-point of meaning because it vaguely and implicitly affirms a quantitative relation, which constitutes a problem for a certain level of geometrical

reject it. As a rule, so far as I can judge, he leaves the two conceptions of 'truth' standing side by side, without recognizing their incompatibility. He does not succeed in freeing the 'truth' of mediate thinking from its dualistic implications, or in reducing it to a mere provisional stage of the complete conception of 'truth' as intuitive.

knowledge. It denies that between the diagonal and the side there is a quantitative relation which can be expressed in terms of a common unit; but the denial is significant, because it implies that there is a quantitative relation *of some kind*. It is not a meaningless or an 'infinite' negation (like e. g. 'the diagonal is not hot'), because its negative form conceals a challenge to recognize this unfamiliar relation, and to attempt its determination by new methods.

And if we speak of the 'real counterpart' of such a judgement, its 'reality' is of a most ambiguous and imperfect kind. A hypothetical judgement, or a *rudimentary* disjunctive, expresses a 'real counterpart' in much the same sense and at much the same level. In the gradual development of a science, the mind begins by occupying a region of inquiry with a disjunctive, whose alternatives are shadowy and abstract. It maps out a sphere, so to say, into light and shade, which (when the system of knowledge is fully articulate) will reveal itself as an ordered scale of different colours. It begins with 'either A or not-A', and passes into 'either A or B', where the A defines (whilst it excludes) B, and the B (in its distinction from A) throws A's positive character into relief. Or again, it provisionally isolates certain features, and formulates the consequences flowing from such abstractions; or it may proceed gradually towards a definite affirmation through tentative circumscriptions of the field of inquiry, removing suggested predicates and relations one by one. Such levels of developing knowledge appear in the form of abstract hypothetical and disjunctive judgements, and of negations approximating to bare exclusions. They are knowledge in the making; and their 'counterpart' is reality emerging, not yet fully manifest. The square with its internal differences, its plurality of elements and their reciprocal relations, forms a relatively coherent system, standing out with a certain self-dependence or individuality. But the square, in this its 'reality', is the 'counterpart' of full geometrical knowledge ; and the 'counterparts' of the first rough judgements no more constitute elements within the 'real' square than those judgements themselves survive unmodified in the system of geometrical science.

But there is a sense in which 'the real' is undoubtedly negative, and in which every system of knowledge, however complete, must include negative judgements. For in any genuine whole the constituents cohere in and through their differences. The pieces of a puzzle e. g. combine just in so far as they supplement one another. Each excludes the others in space, each contributes what the others do not, and all together fill in the extended unity of the whole. The puzzle, as a definitely-shaped whole, is a unity of many pieces, which stand out from one another even in their combination ; and the edges by which they unite are also the edges which mark them off from one another. And in a more developed type of systematic whole—a whole whose unity is a balanced order of movements, or a planned co-operation of functions—the negative element is no less essential, perhaps more conspicuous. Such a whole (like e. g. the Solar System, an animal organism, or a State) maintains its being in so far as the parts co-operate to fulfil a determinate scheme of functions. And such co-operation is essentially also division of labour and differentiation of functions. And even where the whole is present in all its parts, and 'exclusion' with its suggestion of spatial separation no longer applies, the parts express the whole with different 'emphases'; and the difference of emphasis is essential, and is a negative element. For otherwise the supposed

'whole' would have collapsed into blank identity—
an identity which, *qua* not distinguished from anything, would itself have no positive character. If then
we place a systematic whole on one side as the 'real
counterpart', and a full systematic knowledge on the
other as its 'representation', the differentiation of the
parts (or of their functions or their 'emphases') is as
vital a characteristic of 'the reality' as their positive
natures; for their distinction from one another, or
what they determinately *are not*, is but one side of
what they positively *are*. And the systematic knowledge, which is to represent this 'reality', will include
negative as well as affirmative judgements on the same
level of significance. Such negations would not
barely exclude, or vaguely imply a positive *to be
revealed* by the advance of knowledge. They would,
in and by their denials, throw into relief the positive
aspect of the 'otherness' which they emphasize; just
as the affirmations within the system would also
negate, inasmuch as they would affirm *precisely*, i.e. so
as to reveal the distinctions of that which they affirm
from its 'others'.

§ 51. Let us make a fresh start in our inquiry by
returning to a point which emerged in the above discussion. We drew attention to a somewhat paradoxical result, which seemed to follow from the distinction
between *A*'s error, as it is *for A while he is in error*, and
as it is *for B*, or for *A* himself when he is aware that
he was in error. So long as I am genuinely in error,
it is essential (or so we thought) that I should believe
myself to be thinking truly. As soon as I recognize
that I am in error, or the moment that I even doubt
whether I may not be in error, I have passed beyond
error itself and am on the road to truth.[1]

Before proceeding in this line of inquiry, I must

[1] Above, pp. 131, 132.

endeavour to dispose of an objection which threatens to block the way altogether. For we may be told ' You are committing an elementary blunder. The state of mind of the erring person is a purely psychological question, and has nothing to do with the nature of error. *That* is a problem for Logic, or Theory of Knowledge, or (if you insist on adopting a certain attitude) for Metaphysics. In the progress of philosophy the concrete subject-matter has been mapped out into different departments. Each department is constituted by the abstracting hypothesis, within which a distinct branch of philosophy works. Thus Psychology and Logic (in the ordinary sense of the term) have become "special sciences". Each works within a different selective hypothesis, and each is concerned with a different aspect of the concrete fact of error. Your attempt to set aside this division, and to consider the concrete fact " in the lump ", can result in nothing but confusion.'

Confusion results, I should agree, if you first map out the territories, and then neglect the divisions which you have made. And confusion also results if you obstinately persist in following a faulty map. ' Are you so certain,' I should ask, ' that your division of territories is right ? Is it not somewhat ominous that the Logic and Psychology, which have grown up within your demarcations, are confronted with problems which appear to be insoluble, and lead back to ultimate positions conflicting with views which your own Metaphysics refuses to modify ?[1] And, after all, I am asking for a very moderate concession, and the risk of confusion is mine and not yours. For all that I propose, is to set aside *provisionally* the current maps ; and to examine the fact of error without prejudice, *as if* the divisions in question were not accepted.'

[1] Cf. above, §§ 43, 44.

We are then to consider A's error, as it is for A whilst he is completely in error. A, let us suppose, judges that the sun rises and sets and travels round the earth. This is a description of certain phenomena as they appear to A, an observer on the earth's surface; and A need not 'err' in so judging. For he may be ignorant of astronomy and aware of his own ignorance, and so make no pretence in his judgement to express the nature of the sun and its relation to the earth. Or he may know that the geocentric system is no longer tenable as an adequate theory of the astronomical facts; and so his judgement may be to him a mere provisional description of certain phenomena, whose full explanation he is content to leave in suspense. He may think of the sun rising and setting, and thus interpret what he sees; but he need not for a moment suppose that the content of his judgement is to survive as such, and without serious alteration, within the coherent system of astronomical science. Or, lastly, he may make the judgement with a full knowledge of its significance, and of the qualifications under which it could claim truth. The meaning of his judgement would *for him* depend upon a background of the fullest astronomical and optical knowledge. And as a thought within that coherent context, or as informed by the 'appercipient character' of a mind at that level of development, his judgement would express for him the way in which the ordered changes in the relative positions of sun and earth *must* appear, under the determinate conditions of vision, to a human observer at a determinate time and place.[1]

If we suppose A to pass through the various stages which we have just sketched, he will be advancing from unpretending simplicity through doubt and tentative suggestion to knowledge. But at no stage of

[1] Cf., perhaps, Spinoza, *Ethics*, ii. 17 Schol., ii. 35 Schol.

his progress will his condition be genuine error. At the outset, his judgement expresses what appears to him ; it professes to be no more, and it is no less. He is, as it were, wandering along a path chosen for his own pleasure ; and it *is* pleasant. He is not under the delusion that he is exploring the country of astronomy. And when, in the second stage, the outlines of that country loom up more definitely before his mind, he is aware that its inner features are to him still uncertain. He makes his judgement tentatively, with the suggestion that, in selecting this path, he may perhaps be opening up a high road in the unknown country. But he knows that he may be mistaken : and *with this knowledge* the 'mistake' (if so it prove) is not an 'error'. And when, finally, the whole country lies plain before him, both in the inner net-work of its roads and in its relations to neighbouring territories, he will recognize the exact bearings of the path he has chosen. In the whole course of his journey he has never 'mistaken' one road for another, in the sense of 'mistake' which commits and misleads. He has never walked along a path, which was to end in a morass, under the confident expectation of reaching a town.

But if *A*'s condition is to be genuine error, his 'mistakes' must commit and mislead. He must plunge into the wrong road with the untroubled certainty that it is right. He must judge that the sun rises and sets and travels round the earth, without a doubt that he is expressing full astronomical truth ; or, if he has doubted, he must have returned to certainty with the added confidence of reflection. *A*'s judgement attains to its full stature of falsity only within his conviction that his judgement expresses the truth neither more nor less ; and in the unfolding of that conviction *A*'s error emerges in its full character as the enemy of knowledge. For *A*'s conviction will unfold itself (if he be an astronomer) as a system of theory which may bar the way for ages to the advance of knowledge, or (if he be a dignitary of the Roman Catholic Church) in the endeavour to save Galileo's soul by threatening to burn his body.

Error, if the above account is right, is that form of ignorance which poses, to itself and to others, as indubitable knowledge; or that form of false thinking which unhesitatingly claims to be true, and *in so claiming* substantiates and completes its falsity.[1]

§ 52. 'But surely,' it will be said, 'there are judgements which are false under any circumstances, and any one who makes them is in error. All judgement, whether true or false, involves a subjective certainty, which is belief in its truth; but this does not affect the question. If I judge that $2 + 3 = 6$, or that the sun goes round the earth, my judgement is false and I am in error. And if I avoid the error by judging under certain mental reservations, that does not mean that a false judgement is no error if it be made without belief. It means simply that I am making different judgements. I am in fact judging that $2 + 3$ *under certain fantastic qualifications* are 6, or that the sun, *considered from a certain point of view*, goes round the earth.'

There is at first sight an attractive simplicity in this way of putting the matter; but it will not stand against our previous conclusions.[2] It assumes—what we have seen to be untenable—that a judgement can

---

[1] Cf. Plato, *Sophist.*, 229 C:

ΞΕ.   Ἀγνοίας γοῦν μέγα τί μοι δοκῶ καὶ χαλεπὸν ἀφωρισμένον ὁρᾶν εἶδος, πᾶσι τοῖς ἄλλοις αὐτῆς ἀντίσταθμον μέρεσιν.

ΘΕΑΙ. Ποῖον δή;

ΞΕ.   Τὸ μὴ κατειδότα τι δοκεῖν εἰδέναι· δι' οὗ κινδυνεύει πάντα ὅσα διανοίᾳ σφαλλόμεθα γίγνεσθαι πᾶσιν.

[2] Cf. above, §§ 31 ff.

express determinate meaning, and be true or false, in isolation from the context within which it is formulated, or without reference to the 'appercipient character' of the mind which makes it. The judgement '$2 + 3 = 6$' is no more false as such and in itself than a road is wrong *per se* and without reference to the object of the traveller. There are no roads which are such that to take them is *eo ipso* to lose one's way; and there are no judgements so constituted that the person who makes them *must* be in error. The judgement '$2 + 3 = 6$' is false because its meaning is part of a context of meaning, and a part which collides with the other parts. The judgement is really '$2 + 3$ conceived under the conditions of the numerical system $= 6$'; and the collision, the falsity, and the error attach to the judgement *qua* brought into connexion with the system of judgements thus implied. There is neither collision, falsity, nor error, in so far as the mind holds this element in suspense against the remainder of the significant context of its scientific thinking; or, again, in so far as the mind, by extending the field of its significant thought, relegates the judgement in question to the sphere of 'fiction' or 'fantastic supposal', i.e. to a sphere of meaning remote from the sphere of scientific thought, and connected therewith by complex mediation. For *then* the judgement is a fragment seeking admission into the ordered whole of thought, prepared to undergo adaptation, and to acquiesce in whatever position may be assigned to it. It is no longer a blustering self-confident assertion, insisting upon the unaltered maintenance of its individual character, and forcing an entrance into *this* determinate sphere of thought.

It is this claim to express truth unqualified—this arrogant self-confidence, with all the consequences to which it may lead—that constitutes the 'sting' of error. For though my error may prove the stepping-stone to fuller knowledge in myself or in others, *my actual being in error* was an insistent belief in the completeness of my partial knowledge. And this, with all the mischief that it may have entailed, is a hostile element, which refuses to be worked in as a necessary step in the advancement of knowledge; just as, though I may emerge from crime and sorrow and suffering a nobler and a wiser character, the actual pain of the suffering, and the actual degradation of the crime, are positive evils not to be conjured away, nor to be resolved into lesser stages in the development of the greater good. If the only road to truth and goodness lies through error and crime, it is not *prima facie* the most direct conceivable.[1] Tacking may be the only method of sailing against an unfavourable wind; but the advance is slow for all that, and cumbrous, and involves loss of way at every tack. Or—and this is a metaphor more closely fitted to the facts—to be tossed from rock to rock across a chasm is one way of reaching the bottom; but it is neither the shortest, nor the most painless, nor necessarily the least dangerous, route.

Though, therefore, it be admitted that *A*'s error is an error *to him* only when it is over, and *to others* only in so far as they comprehend it as a harmless 'moment' within a wider knowledge; error is not thereby reduced to 'a superseded stage in the development of truth.'[2] For precisely that feature in error, which

---

[1] I have not hesitated to speak of moral evil and crime, and again of suffering and sorrow, as in some sense parallel in their respective spheres to error; and I have made a free use of them as illustrations. But I cannot here enter more fully into the analysis of these manifestations of the 'negative element'. The problem of error is more than enough to occupy me. And if my hasty references to these other forms of the negative are misleading, I can but apologize to the reader, and beg him to treat them as withdrawn.   [2] Cf. above, p. 131.

at the time robs it of its sting for the erring person
(viz. his untroubled confidence in the truth of his
judgement), constitutes the distinctive character of
error and its power for mischief. And this feature
is never annulled and never converted into an element
of the fuller knowledge. The triumphant development
of astronomy has neither annulled nor absorbed the
persecution of Galileo; nor has the growth of a
nation's well-being wiped out the blood and the suffering of those who fought for its liberty, or rendered
unfelt the bitter bereavement of their wives and
children.

§ 53. Undoubtedly there is a sense in which error is
nearer to truth than blank ignorance, and crime is
morally an advance on the innocence which is without
'the knowledge of good and evil'. Undoubtedly, again,
a mind may through error have solidified and rendered
more concrete the substance of its knowledge, and a
will may have emerged from crime to a firmer grasp
and a fuller realization of the moral ideal; and (for
all I know) an animal organism may, by conquering
disease, have heightened and extended its vitality. But
when all this has been admitted and properly emphasized, error and crime still stand out as more, and as
other, than partial knowledge and imperfect goodness;
and the feature on which I am insisting still remains
unaccounted for, and indeed unrecognized. The problem of error has not been solved, because error itself
has never been seized at all. Error itself—the defiant
and uncompromising enemy—slipped through our
fingers before they closed to grasp the area of inquiry.

The above remarks apply, if I am not mistaken, to
some not uncommon attempts to formulate a solution
of the problem of error in the terminology of aesthetics.
A work of art—e. g. a picture, or still more obviously
a musical composition—is, as it were, a miniature

significant whole; and the character of its coherence is beauty. A musical masterpiece is essentially a self-fulfilment, which moves through opposition and contrast, and which in that self-contained movement makes and maintains its coherent individuality. The opposition and the contrast, as moments in the process, simply enrich the concrete individuality of the whole. Chords which, *if the movement were arrested*, would be discords (i. e. *aesthetically* hostile and ugly), within the self-fulfilment of the whole significance contribute to the increased fullness and grandeur of the harmony. Hence it has become a commonplace to say that, in a picture or a piece of music, the richness of the colouring and the fullness of the harmony depend upon the violence of the contrasts; and we are asked to view error and crime as discords which are resolved in the harmony of truth and goodness, or as contrasts which enrich and give concrete substance to the significant wholes of knowledge and conduct. In the work of art, none of the contrasting features stand out in glaring hostility. As hostile and as ugly, they *are* not any longer; and so, in the perfection of knowledge and conduct, error and crime *as such* are not at all. And having conceded so much, we must surely go further. For *outside* the unity of a work of art there is neither aesthetic beauty nor ugliness. No chord, as such and in itself, is aesthetically discordant or ugly; and no colour, in and for itself, can have aesthetic predicates. Similarly, an action which, *within* the coherent system of reasonable purpose, intensifies the realization of the moral ideal by its contrast-effect, *outside* that system (where its hostility would have free play) is not capable of receiving moral predicates at all. And the 'error', which *within* the coherent system of knowledge is stripped of its hostility, and has become a necessary 'moment' in the self-revelation of the truth, *outside* that system rejects all logical predicates, and is neither true nor false. And with this the solution may seem to be accomplished ; for error and crime have as such been removed altogether.

But the coherent systems of knowledge or of goodness, within which error and crime thus disappear, are not the one significant whole whose character is (for the coherence-notion) truth. They are subordinate wholes, relatively-coherent systems, constituted by a selecting and abstracting hypothesis within the complete whole ; and it is a mark of their abstractness that certain elements appear within them not at all, or only in a mutilated form. Error, I am maintaining, is distinctively characterized by a discordance and a hostility which debar it from becoming merely a contrasting element within the developing system of knowledge. In being treated as such a vanishing contrast, it is stripped of that which makes it what it essentially is, and it loses the very feature which constitutes the problem for Metaphysics. If we draw our examples from the contrasting differences and the opposing elements within a work of art, and talk of resolving discords into a fuller harmony, we must not forget that the opposition, which constitutes the problem of error, is deeper and more radical than the mere contrast between lesser and fuller stages of knowledge. Within the harmony of knowledge there is no discordant element possessed of the genuine ugliness of error. Error, as it calls for explanation, is a ' discord ' which is resolved, if at all, only within the self-fulfilment of the one significant whole.

§ 54. If the above argument is right, we have encountered, as a distinctive feature within the fact of error, a discordance too radical to be resolved into harmony within the development of knowledge. What is the exact basis or principle of this discordance? If we can answer this question, we may find ourselves face to face with that 'ultimate opposition in the heart of things,' that 'negative element in reality,' of which we are in search.

But before we can advance, we must remove a certain vagueness in our position. As against the crude dualism of the correspondence-notion, and the still cruder pluralism which conceived truth as a quality of independent entities, we are committed to some form of monism. For the coherence-notion is essentially monistic; and though we have found problems within that notion which we are unable to solve, we have not yet abandoned the attempt to mould it into a form in which it may overcome the difficulties. Our treatment of error in the last four sections has assumed the coherence-notion of truth as its basis; but the basis remains at present vague and undeveloped. We have not expressly formulated the problem of error in terms of a systematic theory of truth as coherence; and indeed we have no such systematic theory before us. We examined the views of Aristotle as representing the correspondence-notion; but we have not studied any typical representative of the coherence-notion.

Now the monistic system of Spinoza stands out in the history of philosophy as representing the kind of position which we have been trying to develop and maintain. And if we trace the outlines of Spinoza's theory of the nature of things, and follow him in his endeavour to deal with the problem of error, we shall have corrected the vagueness of our present attitude. For we shall be studying a philosophy in which the notion of coherence obtains definite form and systematic development, and in which there is a masterly effort to reckon with the difficulties. Even if we are forced to admit that error in its full discordance

refuses to fall harmoniously within Reality as he conceives it, we shall at least have obtained a more
definite grasp of the problem. And if we are thus
enabled to disentangle the principle of the discordance
in error, we shall have made a considerable advance.
For *then* we ought to be in a position to see what kind
of remodelling Spinoza's theory would require to meet
the difficulty; and in what way, if in any, his formulation of the coherence-notion could be transformed
into an adequate theory of truth.

If we are to appreciate Spinoza's position, we must
start with his distinction between 'substantial' (or
self-dependent) and 'modal' (or dependent) being.
There is only one self-dependent being or Substance,
viz. the universe in its infinite or all-inclusive single-
ness. All other so-called 'things' follow from it as
the 'effects' of its immanent causality, and are
possessed of derivative or 'modal' reality. In so far as
they are real they are 'modes' (phases, modifications)
of the one Substance. They are not 'in' themselves,
but 'in' Substance.

The one Substance, or 'God', is absolutely single
and absolutely concrete; i. e. God comprises, within
the indivisible unity of his individual being, all
positive characters in which reality is expressed.
Using the term 'Attribute' to mean 'that which
intellect perceives as constituting the essential nature
of Substance [1],' God's infinite concreteness of nature, so
far as it is understood, demands an infinite variety of
Attributes for its expression; or God includes, within
his complete being, absolutely all forms in which
reality can be manifest to intelligence. All the

---

[1] Spinoza, *Ethics*, i, def. 4. I am assuming a certain familiarity
with Spinoza's terminology. Perhaps I may be allowed to refer
the reader to my *Study of the Ethics of Spinoza*, where I have
attempted to establish in detail the interpretation which I am
here stating dogmatically and in outline.

Attributes *together* exhaustively manifest all the aspects of God's essential nature. Each Attribute is 'infinite in its own kind', i. e. exhaustively expresses Substance in one of its essential and ultimate characters. But each Attribute, though thus including the whole of the character which it expresses, excludes all other features of God's essential nature. God, we may say, is revealed *whole* in each Attribute, but *differently* in each, and *wholly* only in all of them together.

Amongst the infinity of Attributes there is one which Spinoza calls *cogitatio*. We may represent this by 'Thought', though (as will be seen) the English term is not an adequate translation. The Attribute of Thought is the 'ideal' side of Substance, and is by its very nature the awareness of itself and of all the other Attributes or sides of God's essential being. God's entire being, we may perhaps say, is reflected upon itself, and this reflectedness is itself one of the ultimate characters of his being, viz. the character expressed in the Attribute of Thought. And since Thought, like every Attribute, is the exhaustive expression of the whole of Substance in one positive aspect of its essential nature, God's Thought is God ideally manifest in his entire completeness; i. e. it is God adequately conscious of himself (viz. of all Reality), and conscious of this consciousness of himself.

We need not concern ourselves further with the infinity[1] of Attributes which together constitute the complete essential nature of God. For to the *human* intelligence, God is manifest under two Attributes only, viz. Extension and Thought. The Universe is manifest to man as a Substance extended in three dimensions, a corporeal or material Substance, and as

---

[1] The difficulties which centre round Spinoza's conception of an infinity of Attributes, perceived by 'intelligence' but unknowable to man, do not specially affect his theory of error.

a Substance instinct with life and consciousness, a psychical, spiritual, or thinking Substance. And the Universe *qua* extended is reflected under the Attribute of Thought, this reflection being also turned upon itself. Hence the Universe *qua* thinking is (for human experience) at once the soul-side of the Universe *qua* corporeal, and the awareness both of itself and of its corporeal ' object '.

We have now to bring out another side of Spinoza's conception of God. God, as the absolutely self-dependent being, is at once cause and effect of himself. As absolutely self-dependent, he is absolutely ' free' or omnipotent ; and the Attributes, in which his essential nature is manifested, are so many lines of force [1] in which his absolute power is actual. Considered as the Substance whose unbroken unity includes an infinity of Attributes, or whose omnipotence acts in an infinity of lines of force, God is *natura naturans*, the ' free ' cause of himself, i. e. of all that is. And considered as the necessary effect of his own free causality, God is *natura naturata*, the system of modes which flow from his being as its necessary consequences. God the cause (*natura naturans*) is the ground of God the effect (*natura naturata*) ; and ' God the effect' is the totality of the necessary modifications of the one Substance, conceived as a coherent system of differences immanent within God's unity. [2] Every mode within this system is a state of God, i. e. a partial manifestation of Substance expressed under *all* the Attributes. [3] Or, for human intelligence, the Universe is articulated as one modal system, every mode of which is both ' Extended' and ' Thinking'. One and the same modal system, with one and the same inner organization (order of sequence or principle of coherence), is *qua* Extended,

---

[1] Cf. e.g. *Ethics*, ii. 1, S.; ii. 7, C.; ii. 21, S.
[2] Cf. *Ethics*, i. 29, S.   [3] Cf. *Ethics*, ii. 7, S.

the world of bodies or the universe of material things ; and, *qua* ' reflected' and ' reflecting', the world of souls or the psychical universe. The modal system thus viewed in its complete coherence, as the totality of the states of Substance conceived *in* Substance, is the time-lessly-actual articulation of God's nature. Each mode, within that system and in its dependence on God, is ' infinite' and ' eternal'. It is ' infinite' because the limitations of its ' essence' are made good by the completing context of the system.[1] And it is ' eternal' because its ' existence' flows necessarily from its ' essence' as thus completed. In this necessary dependence it is ' actual' ; but not in the sense that it occurs in time and space, and endures as an existent object of perception. Its essence is a fragment of God's essence, its timeless self-assertion a partial manifestation of God's omnipotence. God's infinite power, or self-maintenance, shines through all the modes and invests them with eternal actuality or self-affirmation.[2]

The modal system *under the Attribute of Extension* is the corporeal universe viewed as ' one individual, whose parts, i. e. all bodies, exhibit infinite variations without any change of the whole individual.'[3] It is the physical universe, as it would be for the clear thinking of science and philosophy (*ratio* and *scientia intuitiva*), not as it is for the confused picturing of uncritical perception (*imaginatio*) ; not the phenomenal

[1] Cf. e.g. *Ethics*, v. 40, S.
[2] Cf. e.g. *Ethics*, ii. 45, S., v. 29, S. The student of Spinoza will fill in for himself the details which I have omitted here and elsewhere, and will recognize the places where I have passed over thorny questions in silence. It does not seem necessary, for my present purpose, to enter fully into the many difficulties of interpretation which beset Spinoza's conception of the modal system ; nor can I follow out in detail his doctrine of the three grades of apprehension. Though I am far from holding that these are matters of *merely* antiquarian interest, a full discussion of them would take us too far from our present subject.
[3] *Ethics*, ii. Lem. 7, S.

world with its shifting colours and sounds, its apparent contingency and its arbitrary comings into being and passings away, but a system of infinitely diverse motions which maintain, in and through their diversity, one and the same balance of 'motion-and-rest'. And, *under the Attribute of Thought,* it is the completely coherent system of 'ideas' in which the 'infinite intelligence' of God is articulated. Every 'idea', *qua* sustained in that coherent context, is necessarily adequate; or as Spinoza expresses it, 'all ideas as referred to God are true.'[1]

Within the modal system of *natura naturata* every 'idea' (or mode of Thought) is at once the soul-side, and the adequate apprehension, of a mode of Extension. The 'bodies' in which God's Extension is articulated, and the 'ideas' in which his infinite intelligence is expressed, are each of them a determinate, self-maintaining, eternal mode of Substance under two of its Attributes. And, in so far as ' we ' are ' modes ' in this sense, our mind is a timelessly-actual differentiation of the intelligence of God, and is the adequate apprehension of a timelessly-actual differentiation of God's Extension. 'Our' mind is, so far, neither more nor less than a thought of God, and a thought possessed of a certain individuality or self-completeness; and ' our ' body is an essential modification of Extension, which that thought expresses 'under the form of eternity.'[2]

§ 55. It is obvious that this individuality and self-containedness of the modes within *natura naturata* is relative only; and Spinoza recognizes different grades of individuality within the system of Extension, and different grades of self-dependence or ' freedom ' within the ideal expression of the modal system.[3] It is

---

[1] Cf. e.g. *Ethics,* ii. 7, C. and S.; ii. 32 and *dem.*
[2] Cf. *Ethics,* v. 22.
[3] Cf. *Ethics,* ii. 13, S.; iv (on the *homo liber*); v. 38–40 and 40, S.

also obvious that the recognition of *any* individuality—
even a relative self-containedness—within the purely
affirmative being of God, is logically difficult, if not
impossible. And this is a point to which we shall
have to return, as it is here (in the exclusion of the
negative element) that Spinoza's formulation of the
coherence-notion is most open to criticism. But—
assuming for the moment the modal differentiation
of God, with the recognition of grades of relative
self-containedness in the modes—we have still on
our hands the whole phenomenal world, the 'things'
and 'events' of ordinary consciousness.[1] It is
here that the problem of error arises, and here that
Spinoza's theory is in part most successful and in part
most perplexing.

We have seen that the modes as they really are
(viz. as the immanent effects of God's causality) constitute a coherent system, and in that coherence are
yet differentiated and manifest a certain determinate
self-affirmation. There is grave doubt whether Spinoza
is entitled to admit this differentiation; and, setting
that doubt aside, the principle on which the differentiation proceeds is far from clear. But at least we have
no right to assume that anything, which for uncritical
perception (for the picture-thinking of *imaginatio*) appears as 'individual' and as 'one', stands out as
a single mode, as a self-dependent difference, in the
coherent being of God.[2] My conscious 'self' e.g. as
it is for me at any moment of my feeling, and again
my 'body', as it appears to me or another percipient here
and now, are 'actual things' from the point of view of
the 'imaginative' apprehension. But the individuality
and self-containedness, which a confused perceptive
apprehension thus attributes to them, is not necessarily
the self-dependent being which belongs to the clearly-

[1] Cf. *Ethics*, ii. 29, C. and S.; v. 29, S.   [2] Cf. above, p. 61, note.

conceived modes within *natura naturata*. We must
not assume that the 'ideal' elements, of which our
self (as we feel it) is a complex, constitute a single
mode in the Attribute of Thought, or a self-contained
'idea' in the intelligence of God; nor that the
corpuscles, of which my body (as perceived here and
now) is the complex, constitute a single individual
mode in the Attribute of Extension. 'Our mind is
an eternal mode of God's thinking'; but only 'our
mind *quatenus intelligit*'. And 'our' body is an
eternal mode of God's Extension; but only 'our'
body in so far as it is 'an essential nature' expressed
'under the form of eternity' in an 'idea' of God.[1]

But though the 'imaginative' apprehension is
fragmentary and confused, it must (in so far as it is
thinking at all) fall within God's Thought. And the
complex of things and events, as it appears under the
'categories of imagination'[2], must manifest the complete reality of God, however distorted and mutilated
the manifestation may be. For God is all; and all
that 'is', is 'in' God. Hence Spinoza endeavours
to express the world of appearance (the complex of
finite 'things', contingent and transitory 'events')
in terms of God's causality; and to extend his conception, that all human thinking is God thinking in
man, so as to cover even the error and falsity of the
'imaginative' apprehension. The modes within the
coherence of *natura naturata* are possessed of eternal
self-affirmation; and this is their full actuality. But
that full actuality is partially and imperfectly expressed as existence in relation to a determinate place
and time; as the 'actuality' which is duration in the
temporal series, and which characterizes the existent

[1] Cf. *Ethics*, v. 40, S.; v. 22.
[2] '*Auxilia imaginationis*' (time, number, measure); cf. Spinoza,
Ep. 12.

things and events in the phenomenal world.[1] The modes in this partial expression of their full being— in their existence which is temporally and locally limited—are ' finite '; for they have been torn from their completing context, and their being is therefore partly negated.[2] And though, in their finiteness, they are still effects of God's causality, they are effects which depend for their being and occurrence upon an endless chain of antecedent finite modifications of God. Or, as Spinoza expresses it, every single thing, which is finite and has a determinate existence, must have followed from God so far as he is modified by a modification which is finite and has a determinate existence; and similarly this cause or modification must likewise have been determined by another modification of God, which is finite and has a determinate existence; and that by another, and so on *in infinitum.*[3]

Thus, the endeavour to express the world of appearance in terms of God's causality, results in throwing back into the nature of God the negative element, which had been excluded. For the mutilation or partial negation of the modes, which constitutes the characteristic finiteness of the phenomenal things and events as they occur ' in the common order of nature ', re-appears in God, the cause. It is only a God already infected by an endless series of finite modifications who is the cause of the finite; not the God whose infinite being is absolutely affirmative. And it will not help us to

---

[1] Cf. *Ethics*, ii. 8 and C. ; v. 29, S. I am assuming that the ' rerum singularium . . . essentiae formales ', of which *Ethics* ii. 8 speaks, are *not* the modes of *natura naturata* in their full being, but a ' moment ' of their full being which is supplemented by their ' duration ', i.e. their actual existence in time and place. The point is very obscure, and I cannot here defend my interpretation. Cf. my *Study of the Ethics of Spinoza*, pp. 119-22, 221-5.

[2] Cf. *Ethics*, i. 8, S. i ' Quum finitum esse revera sit ex parte negatio . . . existentiae alicuius naturae, . . .'

[3] Cf. *Ethics*, i. 28 and *dem.*

transfer the burden to the 'imaginative' consciousness, as that *for which* God's completely affirmative being 'appears' in the partly negated and mutilated form of an endless series of finites. For 'imaginative' apprehension is itself fragmentary thinking, modes of God's Thought mutilated by being torn out of their coherent context.[1] And so the 'world of appearance' is Reality as it is for an apprehension itself a member of that world ; and the being of the inadequate apprehension presupposes the being of the partly illusory world which it was to condition.

§ 56. We are now prepared to state Spinoza's theory as it applies to the problem of error.

'We,' so far as 'our mind' is clear thinking and 'our body' an essential and eternal differentiation of Extension, are a mode of *natura naturata*. Our mind is a thought of God, and our body is the mode of God's Extension which that thought ideally *is* and adequately apprehends ; and this mode, both *qua* extended and *qua* spiritual, possesses, in its dependence on God, a determinate self-affirmation or individuality which is timelessly actual.

But 'we', as existing in time and place, are members of the world of appearance, modifications of God abstracted from their completing context, finite and without genuine unity or individuality. From this point of view, our soul is the 'idea' of an actually-existing (i.e. temporally-durating) body ; or, rather, our soul is a complex of ideal elements, the 'reflection' of a complex of corpuscles.[2]

God's 'infinite power of thinking' is articulated into the system of self-contained 'ideas', which are

---

[1] Cf. *e.g. Ethics*, ii. 26, C. and *dem.* (with the propositions to which it refers) ; ii. 29, C.

[2] Cf. *Ethics*, ii. 11 (notice specially the demonstration, with its reference to ii. 8, C.) ; ii. 13 and C.; ii. 15.

the 'minds' and the adequate apprehensions of the modes of his infinite Extension. The content of God's infinite intelligence, we may perhaps say, is a significant whole, a concrete meaning expressed in, and as, many thoughts. The single thoughts have their full significance only within the unity of meaning which is the whole intelligence of God; and their singleness or full individuality is actual only in that coherence. Yet some of them at least are possessed of a relative self-containedness which renders them significant in various degrees within their own contents. And so far as a relatively self-contained thought of God constitutes our mind—i. e. enters whole into the content of our thinking, and is whole as our thought—we attain to truth; for God is thinking *in* and *as* our thought.

But God's 'infinite power of thinking' also 'appears' as the endless succession of finite (i. e. fragmentary and mutilated) ideal elements, the soul-side of the endless series of corporeal changes in the world of finite bodies. The changes in the constituent corpuscles of our temporally-existent body, and the ideal changes within our temporally-existent soul which 'reflect' these bodily 'affections', are effects of God's causality mediated by an endless chain of antecedent changes. Though, however, such psychical changes (perceptions, emotions, thoughts) are God thinking *in* us, they are not necessarily God thinking *as* our thought and as that alone. God's thought may be, as it were, *too large* to enter whole and unmutilated into the constitution of our mind. The ideal changes, which are our thoughts, may be mere fragments of a complete thought of God, which is distributed over many different finite minds. When that is so, God's thought constitutes the many different minds together, but appears in each of them severally as a fragmentary, mutilated, and inadequate apprehension.[1] And if a mind, in which God's thought is thus mutilated, fails to recognize the fragmentariness of its apprehension, its apprehension becomes false and is error.

Thus, 'in God' there is no error; for 'in God' all ideas are in their coherent context, and therefore complete and adequate. And the mere partialness or inadequacy of an idea in the human mind does not *of itself* constitute error. For this is a mere absence of a supplementation, a sheer negative exclusion. There is no positive quality in the inadequate idea *as such*, which must be referred to God as a feature of his being. The idea, which *as referred to a particular human mind* is fragmentary and inadequate, in God's Thinking—as distributed over other minds—is complete and adequate. As a mode of God's Thinking, the idea is whole and entire; not a patchwork of many fragments, with barriers of division between them. The idea only becomes error, so far as, in its reference to the particular human mind, it becomes a fragment isolated from its supplementing fragments, and invested in this isolation with an individual self-containedness.[2] *Then* the mutilated fragment of the idea, which is enclosed within the barriers of the particular mind, appears for that mind, in its confident self-assurance, as adequate and whole. 'Falsity consists in the privation of that knowledge which the inadequate (mutilated and confused) ideas involve'[3]; and error in the end depends upon the isolating

---

[1] Cf. *Ethics*, ii. 11, C. '. . . When therefore the human mind is said to perceive this or that, we mean that God, . . . *qua* constituting the essential nature of the human mind, has this or that idea; and when God has this or that idea, not only *qua* constituting the nature of the human mind, but also *qua* possessing the idea of something else along with the human mind, then the human mind is said to perceive a thing only partially or inadequately.'

[2] Cf. *Ethics*, ii. 32-4, 36 and *dem.*   [3] *Ethics*, ii. 35.

self-assertion, whereby the finite mind, failing to recognize its own incompleteness, is for itself an independent and self-contained individual.

§ 57. Spinoza, if the above exposition is substantially correct, seizes error in its distinctive character and in its full discordance; but in this full discordance error will not fit coherently into his system.

Incomplete or fragmentary thinking, he rightly insists, is not *as such* false; nor is the mind, through which the complete truth obtains partial expression, thereby in error. God's 'infinite intelligence' (the modal system under the Attribute of Thought) is articulate in and as the single 'thoughts', which constitute the several 'minds' in their eternal being. Thus the fullness of knowledge, which God *is* as reflected on himself, is a concrete unity of meaning self-affirmed in a plurality of different contributory thoughts, or as a plurality of different individual minds. Each mind is a 'part' only of the complete intelligence, each thought a fragmentary expression of the whole meaning. But it is the whole meaning, the one substantial significance, which is partially expressed in each; and the partial expressions are the different 'emphases' which its self-affirmation demands. And since every mode of Thought reflects not only a mode of Extension, but also itself, the one substantial significance is turned upon itself in each of its modal differences: i.e. the 'infinite intelligence' is drawn into itself in each of its 'parts'. Every thought of God, within the coherent context which it contributes to constitute, is thus 'for itself', a self-contained individual mind.

So far we might be content to accept the substance of Spinoza's doctrine, whilst modifying the letter of some of his statements. For if the modes of *natura naturata* are thus 'for themselves' in their absolute dependence on God, God's being is no longer 'purely affirmative', unless the 'purely affirmative' essentially includes articulate diversity. And if the one significance, in affirming itself in all its different 'emphases', affirms itself uniquely in each of them, so that each draws for itself a distinctive individuality in the affirmation which unites it with all the others, 'negativity' is essential to the conception of God. The differences within the articulated unity are not indeed 'independent entities' absolutely severed from one another, or tacked together by 'external relations'. But they are genuinely distinct emphases of the one; and in their distinctions, in which they are 'for themselves', they exclude and negate each other. The exclusion and negation, since each mode is completely itself only in its coherence with all, are relative; but they are not illusory, nor do they vanish in the 'affirmative' being of God.

But Spinoza's theory seems to break down when we consider error, i.e. the fragmentary thinking which, claiming to be complete, is false. For error, as he conceives it, involves that an undifferentiated portion of a 'thought' of God—a fragment, which is not in any way marked off within the single 'thought', and is thus not one, not self-contained, not 'a' fragment at all—yet *is* 'for itself', and affirms itself as self-contained and individual. He speaks as if 'a single thought' of God, which is distributed over many different 'minds', appears mutilated within one of these 'minds'. And this mind hedges in the mutilated fragment with the barriers of its own illusory individuality, and with an illusory self-assurance confuses it with the whole thought, and thus is in error.

But 'a mind', according to his theory, is nothing but a thought of God reflected on itself; and if the thought is undivided and one and without inner plurality, its self-reflection is *one* mind, and not a plurality of minds. Thus the *many* different minds, constituted by *a single* thought of God, have no distinctive being at all. Their plurality and the self-assurance of each or of any of them, are sheer inexplicable illusions, for which Spinoza's theory can assign no real basis. Or if their plurality is real, the thought distributed over them is itself many, and not one. And on either alternative the supposed explanation of error vanishes.

Error, no doubt, is an illusory appearance of knowledge, and involves in the end an illusory assumption of self-containedness and individuality. But where, within Spinoza's conception of God, is the ground of the illusion? Partial negation and severance constitute the finiteness of the modes, and the self-affirmation of the modes in this mutilation is the basis of error. But a negation which severs the modes from their coherence, and a self-assertion of that which has no distinct being, are inconceivable within Spinoza's metaphysical system.

We have thus confirmed the stress which we laid upon this self-assertive feature in error. The erring subject's confident belief in the truth of his knowledge distinctively characterizes error, and converts a partial apprehension of the truth into falsity. It is this feature which refuses to be absorbed in fuller knowledge, and which makes the fact of error a problem for Metaphysics. And we have traced this discordance in error to its principle as the claim of the finite to self-dependence : a claim which monism, *at least in the form given to it by Spinoza*, cannot render intelligible. It is possible to insist upon the self-affirmation of the modes *in their dependence*, and to attribute to them a self-contained individuality in so far as the one Substance is expressed differently, uniquely emphasized, in each of them. But error involves that the modes contrive somehow to 'be' *apart from their coherence*, and to set themselves up in isolation from one another and against their substantial unity. And this declaration of independence, where that which declares is nothing real and nothing real is declared, is unthinkable.

§ 58. Long ago—almost at the outset of our inquiry —we drew attention to what we called 'the dual nature of human experience'. We distinguished a certain timeless independence and universality, and on the other hand a manifestation in and for finite individuals, through temporal processes and under temporal conditions. We spoke of this distinction as familiar, and we treated the indissoluble union of these contrasting aspects as the fundamental character of our experience : i.e. we took it rather as the ground for explaining other things than as something itself requiring, or admitting of, explanation. Truth, beauty, goodness, are timeless, universal, independent structures ; and yet also it is essential to them to be manifested in the thinking of finite subjects, in the actions and volitions of perishing agents, in and through the emotions and the creative activities of individual artists and lovers of art.[1] The composer e. g. 'discovers' or 'makes' a melody ; 'calls into being' or 'finds'—the two sets of terms together express the fact—a living organized structure of harmony or beautiful sound. And the work of art which he has brought to birth, while it lives in being played and heard, and is actual in the emotions of finite subjects, is yet a thing of transcendent value, independent, universal, and timeless in its beauty. Composer, players, and audience are mere instruments for the manifestation of its being, and 'it' controls their service and compels their worship. Thus lovers

[1] Cf. above, § 7.

'create' and also 'discover' a living structure of love, which controls their lives and uses them as the instruments of its being. They can neither annihilate it at will, nor compel it to be. Yet it has come to birth in them, it draws the breath of its life in their feelings, volitions, and actions, and with the changes of their finite individualities it may vanish in estrangement or enmity. So the man of science, or the philosopher, labours to discover the truth; i. e. to find articulated before him an organized structure of knowledge. And when he 'makes the discovery' (the very phrase is suggestive), he finds something timeless and unalterable, which is independent of himself and all individual inquirers, and controls for ever all finite thinking. Yet its being is essentially 'in' and 'for' and 'as' the temporal and finite thinking of the individual minds. It is universal; but its universality is stamped with the unique differences of the many minds, in whose thinking it is manifest. It is independent and dominates our thought; but it is *in* and *as* our thinking that its controlling independence is exercised.

You will say, perhaps, that all this is a needless confusion, which may be avoided by a very simple distinction. The artist and the man of science make beautiful things and true theories; but beauty and truth themselves *are*, and in no sense are made. The aspect of independence, universality, and timelessness falls on one side as the character of certain contents, certain entities, which 'are', but do not 'exist'. And the aspect of finite, temporal, and contingent manifestation falls on the other side, and in no sense enters into the 'being' of goodness, beauty, or truth.

Undoubtedly, a theory of knowledge, conduct, or art, must rule out as irrelevant *some* of these temporal and finite conditions; and I shall return to this point immediately. But if you mean precisely what you say—and otherwise your simple distinction will not have cleared away the supposed 'confusion'—you are demanding a severance which will not stand a moment's reflection. The works of Beethoven, e.g., or of Shelley, were 'beautiful' before the public admired them, and will remain 'beautiful' even though its taste degenerates. Were they beautiful— *were* they or their beauty at all—before Beethoven or Shelley composed them? and will they or their beauty *be*, if (or when) European music is as dead as the music of the ancient Greeks, and English has become a forgotten language? The beauty which *is*, but in no sense *exists* or is manifest, is a very empty abstraction. It is the beauty of a piece of music which is not composed, or heard, or read; of a picture which is not conceived, or seen, or remembered; of a poem neither written, nor thought, nor appreciated. Beauty of this kind is all one, and all (if you like) 'eternal'; and *what* it is, and *what* its 'being' is, is not hard to say. It is a sheer abstraction, without enough content to distinguish it from nothing; and its 'being' is to be the empty object of an empty thought.

And if you insist that at least it is otherwise with truth, and that e. g. the internal angles of a triangle were together equal to two right angles in the days of Adam, or even before, and will remain so when the whole race of man has perished; I am ready in a sense to accept what you say, but I should make a suggestion as to its interpretation. What we *now* recognize as true, is invested *in our present recognition* with a timeless application. We cannot think of a triangle, or indeed of the extended world, without inevitably recognizing *this* as a feature in its character, which is independent of our choice and timelessly (i. e. indifferently through all times) the same. And this 'eternity', which characterizes truth, is manifest *in* and *through* and *as* our present grasp of the nature of things; and is thus a convincing instance of that 'indissoluble union of contrasting aspects' which I am trying to enforce.[1]

§ 59. A theory of knowledge must rule out as irrele-

[1] To say that beauty, truth, and goodness 'are', and that their 'being' has nothing to do with 'existence'; that they are 'real', whether or not they appear in finite experience and under temporal conditions: this, I am maintaining, is to make a barren distinction and to play idly with words. And we can see that this is so, if we will but ask ourselves *what* beauty, *what* truth, and *what* goodness 'are' in absolute severance from the existent, and what kind of 'being' they thus enjoy. But on the other hand, it is fatal to over-emphasize the aspect of 'existence', and there is grave danger of misinterpretation. For are we to say that these structures 'are' not at all, when not yet (or no longer) actual in and as the thoughts, volitions, and emotions of finite subjects? If so, what becomes of their universal, timeless, and independent character? We are disquieted with the thought that, in being discovered, they are 'called into life'; and that, when their finite vehicles vanish, they too sink back into the void within which they were 'found' or 'made'. And unable to acquiesce in this conclusion, we may be tempted to substantiate the finite subjects, and to postulate their everlasting persistence: a 'personal immortality', where our conception of the 'persons' and of their 'survival' is equally confused. Or we may clothe our ignorance in the garb of religion, and postulate a God who sustains in heaven the structures which have fled from earth.

Certainly our experience is full of perplexities, which it is not easy—perhaps not possible—to interpret in terms of a rational theory. We shrink from the charge of scepticism, and are too often afraid to confess the limits of our knowledge. Have we ever convinced ourselves that the death of a friend *in no way* injures the reality of those eternal structures, in the sustaining of which he lived and worked and made 'himself'? And should we be right, if we were convinced? Or who has not felt a jarring sense of loss—a suspicion that something of transcendent value is over and done with—at the conclusion of a noble rendering of a drama or a piece of music? And when one reflects on the nations which have vanished across the stage of history, to all appearance carrying with them structures of transcendent value—the truth, goodness, and beauty, which lived in them, and in which they lived—it seems but cold comfort to be told that fragments of these structures survive in the present; or that e.g. the spirit of Athenian sculpture, poetry, and philosophy, still breathes its influence in modern civilization, and inspires our art and science. At the best, we feel, something of transcendent value is lost; or, if sustained *somehow* in the timeless actuality of 'ideal experience', the *how* eludes the grasp of our rational thinking.

vant *some*—perhaps *most*, but certainly not *all*—of the
temporal and finite conditions under which the truth
is known. The known truth, as the subject of study
in a theory of knowledge, is a concrete universal
content, a single meaning differentiated into many
constituent meanings, and emerging in and for many
different minds. But the constituent meanings are
themselves universal. They are determinate 'judgements of science', or systems of such judgements,
not *this* or *that* opinion. And the 'many different
minds' are different types of 'appercipient character',
different stages and levels of 'the scientific mind';
not the uniquely individual differences of appercipient
character, which distinguish *my* mind from *yours*, nor
the different stages in the temporal growth of the
individual thinker's apprehension. The development
of knowledge from this point of view is not a temporal,
but a logical process : and error finds its place there as
a partial phase or 'moment' in the timeless dialectic,
which is the articulation of the truth.

The differences of *this* and *that* knowing mind—*a
fortiori*, the confused mass of idiosyncrasies which
together distinguish *this* 'person' or 'self' from *that*—
are recognized only to be set aside and, if necessary,
discounted. They are accidental imperfections, superficial irregularities, in the medium through which
truth is reflected; limitations in the vessels through
which knowledge is poured. And the temporal processes of our knowing are mere incidents in the manifestation of truth. They are, so to say, bubbles on
the stream of knowledge ; and the passing show of
arbitrary variation, which they create on the surface,
leaves the depths untroubled—a current uniform and
timeless. My and your thinking, my and your 'self',
the particular temporal processes, and the extreme
self-substantiation of the finite 'modes' which is error

in its full discordance : these are incidents somehow
connected with the known truth, but they themselves,
and the manner of their connexion, are excluded from
the theory of knowledge. They are problems to be
discussed, if anywhere, in Metaphysics. *There* indeed
they force themselves upon us with relentless impor-
tunity. For, to all appearance, the truth 'is' only as
coming to be in and through temporal processes, and
as reflected through the innumerable variations of the
finite minds. The stream of knowledge, it would
seem, must be poured through *these* imperfect vessels,
and cannot flow without breaking into *these* bubbles.
The finite mind, in its knowing activities, is nothing
but *this* emphasis, *this* imperfect expression of the
universal content ; but *this* emphasis is different from
the others, and in its difference and uniqueness essential to the complete expression of the one significance. The temporal process is nothing but a limited
and arrested portion of the timeless actuality ; yet the
latter essentially maintains itself through all and every
determinate portion of time. And if all this is mere
appearance, an illusory seeming, Metaphysics must
show the ground of the illusion in the reality which
is distorted in the appearance.

'But surely,' it will be said, 'all this is beside the
point. The problems connected with the dual character
of knowledge exist only for Metaphysics, and Metaphysics may be trusted to deal with them. A theory
of knowledge, as you yourself have admitted, studies
the known truth *qua* timeless and universal ; and the
temporal and individual aspect of knowledge, if not
entirely eliminated, fades into the background.'

Now I will not pause to contest this objection. I
have admitted that a theory of knowledge is bound to
restrict the area of its inquiry, by abstracting from
' some, or perhaps most, of the temporal and finite

conditions under which the truth is known.' And I will not here question the objector's interpretation of that admission, nor press him to explain more definitely how, on his view, a theory of knowledge is related to Metaphysics. I will assume that a theory of knowledge is a partial science, with a province thus limited and thus severed from Metaphysics ; and that it is entitled to appeal to Metaphysics for the solution of any problems connected with that side of knowledge, which its abstracting hypothesis has discarded. And all I will say is this : *no theory of truth formulated under the coherence-notion is a 'theory of knowledge' in that sense.* For truth, as conceived under the coherence-notion, is the character of the one significant whole ; and a theory of truth thus conceived is of necessity a metaphysical theory. Hence, if the coherence-notion is to be maintained, we cannot exclude these problems, and we cannot shift the burden by an appeal to an extraneous Metaphysics. We must be able to conceive the one significant whole, whose coherence is perfect truth, as a self-fulfilment, in which the finite, temporal, and contingent aspect receives its full recognition and its full solution as the manifestation of the timeless and complete ; and we must be able to show *both* the extreme opposition (which constitutes the discordance of error), *and* the overcoming of it, as essential moments in that self-fulfilment. The absolute individuality of God (to borrow Spinoza's terminology) demands for its self-fulfilment that its modes should be or become 'independent' in a sense which, *at least for themselves and for any experience short of God's absolute experience*, sets them in opposition, hostility, and discord to one another and to their own substantial being. And it demands also that this opposition—or, if it be illusory, the real ground of it—should be an essential contributory moment in the complete self-fulfilment.

§ 60. Let me recapitulate the considerations which have led us to our present position. ' Coherence ' is not to be interpreted as ' formal consistency '. Coherence of form, irrespective of the matter cohering, is mere ' validity ' : at most a negative condition (or *sine qua non*) of the complete truth, which the coherence-notion professes to grasp. The ' coherence ', which is truth, is the concrete character of a significant whole, in which form and matter cannot be severed from one another, nor intelligibly considered apart.[1] And nothing short of the one all-inclusive significant whole —ideal or absolute experience—can be completely ' coherent ' in this sense of the term.[2] Hence truth for the coherence-notion is the character of ideal or absolute experience ; and any partial experience (e. g. human knowledge) is ' true ' more or less, according as it exhibits a character more or less approximating to the complete coherence, or according as ideal experience reveals itself more or less perfectly in it, as the substance of which it is a modal expression.

A theory of truth as coherence, if it is to be adequate, must be an intelligible account of the ultimate coherence in which the one significant whole is self-revealed ; and it must show the lesser forms of experience, with their less complete types of coherence, as essential constitutive ' moments ' in this self-revelation. Thus, it must *render intelligible* the ' dual nature of human experience ', which a mere ' theory of knowledge ', and a theory of art or conduct, *assume* as the fundamental character of the subject-matters which they have respectively to study. It must show e. g. how the complete coherence, which is perfect truth, involves as a necessary ' moment ' in its self-maintenance the self-assertion of the finite modal minds : a self-assertion, which in its extreme form is Error. It

[1] Above, §§ 25, 26.　　　[2] Above, § 27.

must reconcile this self-assertive independence with the modal dependence of the self-asserting minds ; and the reconciliation must be clearly manifest as an essential moment in the coherence, which is the life of the one significant whole.

Now it is obvious that the demands thus made cannot be *completely* satisfied by any metaphysical theory. For the complete satisfaction of these demands would be complete truth manifest to itself. And every metaphysical theory, as the outcome of experience which is partial and so far finite, is at best a partial manifestation of the truth, and not the whole truth wholly self-revealed.

The coherence-notion of truth may thus be said to suffer shipwreck at the very entrance of the harbour. It has carried us safely over the dangers and difficulties to which the other two notions succumbed ; but the voyage ends in disaster, and a disaster which is inevitable. For, unless our whole discussion is fundamentally mistaken, the coherence-notion of necessity involves the recognition that certain demands both *must be* and *cannot be* completely satisfied.

And the tale of our disaster is not yet finished. For there remains a problem, on which I have more than once touched, but which during this chapter has slipt into the background. Yet the difficulties which it presents to the coherence-notion are no less formidable than those we have just considered, and are of themselves sufficient to ensure our discomfiture. For truth, as it appears in human knowledge, is distributed over two opposed factors. Our knowledge is thought ' about ' an Other ; and the opposition of the thought and its Other is apparently vital. Truth— i. e. such truth as we attain in judgement and inference —dwells neither in the thought nor in the thought's

Other, but in some sense in the union of the two. And the union, to which we give the name of 'correspondence', demands the independence and opposition of the factors which it unites.[1]

Now we saw long ago that, if the coherence-notion is to approve itself, 'a continuous passage must be shown from that conception of things, which renders the coherence-notion possible, to the dualistic conception which is involved in correspondence.'[2] Otherwise human knowledge remains, for all we can tell, unrelated to ideal experience ; and though we may describe the truth of correspondence as a 'symptom'[3] of perfect truth, the description is a mere matter of faith, which we cannot expect our critics to accept. And again we decided long ago that ideal experience must include within itself a negative element; that there must be in the very heart of truth some form of Otherness, which will justify the relative independence of subject and object within human knowledge.[4] But if we have thus expressed the most admirable intentions, we have hitherto taken not a single step towards their fulfilment. For we have not shown how this self-diremption of the one significant whole is to be conceived. We have not shown how the self-fulfilment, which is the coherence of the One, necessarily and intelligibly involves the emergence and the overcoming of this inner Otherness.

We might indeed attempt to reduce this fresh difficulty to a variety of the first. For we might urge that the opposition of thought and its Other, which fundamentally characterizes human knowledge, is *in the end* a form in which the self-assertion of the finite and the partialness and inadequacy of finite thought appear. We might appeal once more to the theory of Spinoza.

---

[1] Above, §§ 42–4.   [2] Above, p. 120.   [3] Above, p. 17.
[4] Above, pp. 115 ff., 123.

God's complete Thought is fundamentally 'other' than his Extension and the other Attributes; and yet, as God's Thought, it is indissolubly one with them all. In the ideal experience there is the opposition, but the opposition is overcome. So (we might perhaps suggest) our knowledge—which is God thinking in and as us—exhibits the same identity of utterly opposed factors, the same return from self-estrangement. But in so far as we are not fully conscious of our oneness with God—in so far as 'for ourselves' we are not modes of Substance, but self-assertive individual minds—we experience the 'otherness' of thought's object, and not the overcoming of the 'otherness' which is in and for God. And we might add that where we attain to the full consciousness of our modal dependence on God— where we are 'for ourselves' what we are 'for God'— this alienation is overcome for our consciousness. For in *cognitio intuitiva* we know, and, in knowing, *are* what we know. And in this consummation of knowledge, mediation has not been eliminated, but has attained to the explicit completeness of the union which it involves, and has thereby solidified and rendered concrete the content of the 'intuition'. Discursive thinking 'about' an Other has passed into its own fulfilment as the transparent immediacy of intuition in which truth, absolute and complete, is self-revealed.[1]

But here too, as in the treatment of error, Spinoza's theory is fatally defective. The substantial identity of Thought and the other Attributes is stated dogmatically, but not in any sense made intelligible. The God of Spinoza *is* one, and the unity *is* a simultaneity of contrasted Attributes.[2] The one Substance does not fulfil its being through a self-diremption and a return upon self-identity by the negation of this negative. And though the conception of the one

---

[1] Cf. above, p. 58.   [2] Cf. e.g. Spinoza, *Ethics*, i. 10, S.

significant whole, as manifesting and sustaining its unity through an inner process, is *suggested* by Spinoza's insistence that God's ' essence ' is ' power ', there is no attempt to work out the conception.   The otherness of God's Attributes and their identity are postulated. God is a Substance ' consisting of ' an infinite diversity of Attributes.   God is the union of contrasts ; i.e. the receptacle in which they are statically combined, not the life which fulfils itself in the making and overcoming of oppositions.[1]

Thus, even if we succeeded in reducing the problem of the dualism involved in human knowledge to a form of the first problem, we should still be confronted by an unsolved difficulty.   For we should be no nearer to an intelligible conception of this self-diremption of the ideal experience, and the continuous return from this ' Otherness ' which is to constitute its concrete unity. And since all human discursive knowledge remains thought ' about ' an Other[2], any and every theory of the nature of truth must itself be ' about ' truth as its

---

[1] In Spinoza's God the negative element is not overcome, but simply *is not*.   I may here call attention to a minor difficulty in his theory.   God's Thought is the awareness of itself, as well as of the other attributes.   In this reflection upon itself, an *idea* is an *idea ideae*, a mode of thought with *itself* for its object.   Here then—in self-consciousness—thought and its object are absolutely one.   But the unity is an abstract identity, and not the overcoming of its Other by thought's return upon itself.   For whereas, in the thought which reflects a mode of extension, the same mode of Substance maintains its identity in spite of the Otherness of its two expressions ; in the thought which reflects itself, the reflecting and reflected thoughts are the same mode of Substance expressed under the same Attribute (cf. *Ethics*, ii. 21, S.).

[2] I do not wish to sever mediate and immediate thinking ; and I am not saying that discursive or mediate thinking is *in no sense* also intuitive or immediate.   But in judgement and inference the primary emphasis is on the mediate and discursive side.   Knowledge, so far as that is judgement and inference, is primarily and explicitly thinking ' about ' an Other.   And even though discursive thought may find its concentrated fulfilment in immediate or intuitive knowledge, its character of ' Aboutness ' is not thereby eliminated, nor the ' Otherness ' of its object destroyed.

Other ; i. e. the coherence-notion of truth *on its own admission* can never rise above the level of knowledge which at the best attains to the 'truth' of correspondence. Assuming that the coherence-notion of truth is sound, no theory of truth as coherence can itself be completely true, but is at most possessed of a 'truth' which we may believe, but have not proved, to be 'symptomatic' of perfect truth.

§ 61. We may claim at the end of our discussion to have brought the main difficulties, which confront the coherence-notion of truth, into a clear and definite form. We pointed out at the end of Chapter III, that if an adequate theory of truth is to be formulated, the modal nature of the finite subject of knowledge must be more frankly recognized and maintained ; and that the negative element in ideal experience must be shown as the basis and the justification of the opposition of subject and object in human knowledge.[1] We have now seen that the difficulties in the way of a coherence-theory lie (1) in the reconciliation of the modal nature of the finite subjects with their self-assertive independence ; and (2) in the recognition of the individuality of the significant whole as a life timelessly self-fulfilled through an opposition which it creates and, in creating, overcomes. A theory of truth as coherence, we may say, must enable us to conceive the one significant whole so as to satisfy certain requirements. We must so conceive it that it is a timeless actuality, maintaining and fulfilling itself through the setting up within itself of modes, which yet are independent ; and by creating an inner Otherness or duality, which yet is continuously subdued to unity. It must be an essential 'moment' in the Absolute Life that it should invest its modes with self-dependence, and create within itself an opposition

[1] Above, p. 121.

between two factors; and it must be a no less essential 'moment' that it should timelessly take back into its unity the differences thus created, and 'take them back' without destroying them. And further, we must be able to conceive human discursive thinking, with its persistent opposition between subject and object, with its finite and temporal processes and its unresolved discords, as the *arrest* of this timeless and complete actuality: an arrest, moreover, which is itself an essential 'moment' in the life which is ideal experience.[1]

'Yes,' it will be said, 'a theory of truth as coherence must satisfy these requirements; and it must satisfy them as an intelligible theory, i.e. as a theory itself true *qua* coherent. But this, as you have just shown, is not only *de facto* unaccomplished, but is impossible by the very nature of the case. A theory of truth, based on the coherence-notion, is not itself true *qua* coherent; or if true, its truth is a fatal exception which destroys its own basis. No judgement, or system of judgements, can be completely true, if truth

---

[1] Perhaps I ought to explain that in describing ideal experience, here and elsewhere (e.g. §§ 26, 42, 45), as 'dynamic', as a 'process', 'movement', or 'life', I do not mean to suggest that it is *not yet* complete, but is coming to be complete in time. In comparing it to a living thing, the point of the comparison lies in the balance of movements, processes, or functions, which is at any moment what we call the 'life' of the living thing; *not* in the gradual development of the living thing from one moment to another. I am well aware of the difficulties in this conception, and of the inadequacy of these categories (cf. above, §§ 27 and 28). I may add, that to view *the Universe as a whole* as progressing or coming-to-be in time, is to my mind a contradiction in terms. I can attribute no intelligible meaning to an absolute truth, which is not timelessly and eternally *now*, but which *is to be* at some future time; nor to an 'ideal experience', which is to emerge into actuality at a determinate (though perhaps distant) date. The 'Day of Judgement' and 'the future life' are images, which have their value in certain regions of experience; but I have never been able to see that they or their analogues throw any light on the problems of philosophy.

is "coherence"; and therefore the system of judgements (the theory), in which the coherence-notion is most adequately formulated, must still of necessity fail of complete truth. Thus the end of your discussion is not only failure, but your own admission that failure is inevitable. You emerge from your shipwreck in utter destitution, a sceptic naked and unashamed. And do not imagine that you can cover your shame by an appeal to immediate faith, or to the intuition that *somehow* the nature of things does involve these fundamental oppositions, and does subdue them to its unity without destroying them. For you yourself have insisted that immediate intuitive faith of this kind is neither " true " nor " false ", except in so far as it stands, or fails to stand, the test of mediation.'[1]

And from another quarter our disaster will be used to point a moral against us. ' See what comes,' we shall perhaps hear, ' of setting aside the traditional divisions and the accepted maps. If you had held fast to the distinction between the provinces of Logic and Psychology, and if you had kept Metaphysics safe in the region of eternal and unalterable Reality, all this confusion would have been avoided. Truth and falsity, as predicates of the content of thought, would have been disentangled from the psychical machinery and the temporal processes of cognition. Error, as the condition of the erring subject, would have been an interesting study for Psychology, and possibly also for Moral Philosophy. But you, as a Logician, would have been concerned only with the content of the erring subject's thought; and error, thus considered, is but partial knowledge capable of absorption in the fuller truth. And, in your Metaphysical speculations, you would have moved in a region above the finite with its illusions and problems of self-assertion.'

[1] Cf. above, pp. 55–8.

§ 62. Let us consider how we emerge from the wreck, and where we stand. We have acknowledged that no theory of truth as coherence can be completely true; for as a system of judgements, as a piece of discursive knowledge, it must be 'other' than the truth 'about' which it is, and thus it must fail of that concrete coherence which is complete truth. And again, as the knowledge of mind at a determinate level of appercipient character, it must fall short of the complete self-revelation which is absolute truth manifest to itself. But the former imperfection it shares with all possible *theories* of truth or of anything else; and the latter imperfection need not prevent its being *as true as a theory can be*, and more true (more near to complete coherence) than e.g. theories of truth as correspondence or as a quality of independent entities. For these theories also fall short of absolute truth manifest to itself. They too are the knowledge (the discursive thinking) of mind at a determinate level of appercipient character. And we have not retracted the conclusion which we reached as a result of our criticism of them, viz. that they embody a level of appercipient character lower than the level embodied in the coherence-notion. The coherence-notion fails of complete success; but it has carried us further into the heart of the problem than either of the other two notions, and it has maintained itself against difficulties to which they succumbed.[1]

That the truth itself is one, and whole, and complete, and that all thinking and all experience moves within its recognition and subject to its manifest authority; this I have never doubted. My criticism does not touch the immediate recognition of the one truth, nor the immediate recognition of the various judgements and systems of judgement as more or less true,

[1] Above, pp. 64, 65.

i. e. as approximating more or less closely to the one standard. But this immediate experience of the truth remains for me what it was at the outset—a problem. I have examined certain attempts to mediate it, i.e. to raise this immediate certainty to the level of reflective knowledge. And though I have endeavoured to rank them according to their degrees of comparative success, I have been compelled to confess that none of them can be maintained as in the end and in all respects successful. And if I am told that I ought not to have looked for complete and final triumph, but should have acquiesced in partial success, I should reply that this maxim of procedure can have no rational basis, except for the man who has attempted to formulate a complete theory and, in failing, has recognized *that* and *why* such failure is inevitable. I cannot persuade myself that the sharp division between the provinces of Logic and Psychology is justifiable ; nor that the difficulties, which have perplexed me, are irrelevant. Nor do I believe that a sane Metaphysics can leave Logic and Psychology thus delimited and thus severed; or that the Metaphysician is entitled to acquiesce in logical theories, when their success demands that he should accept within the sphere of Logic assumptions which his own metaphysical theory condemns. And if I am wrong, I may at least have done some service, inasmuch as the failure of my present attempt may be used to warn those who, like myself, are tempted to distrust the accepted maps.

To call a man 'a sceptic' is a recognized mode of abuse ; but not every failure to attain a positive result deserves to be thus condemned. A positive result may be bought at too great a cost ; for it may be due to an abstraction which neglects the 'sting' of the problems. And I do not think that, in closing this Essay with a negative result (for in the main I presume that the result is negative), I am guilty of a ' scepticism ' of which I have any cause to be ashamed. I am ending with a confession of ignorance ; but at least I have cleared my mind of much sham knowledge. And I am old-fashioned enough to believe that this achievement is the first requisite for any one who hopes to learn.

INDEX